BFI FILM CLASSIC

· ·

Edward Buscombe
SERIES EDITOR

Colin MacCabe and David Meeker
SERIES CONSULTANTS

Cinema is a fragile medium. Many of the great classic films of the past now exist, if at all, in damaged or incomplete prints. Concerned about the deterioration in the physical state of our film heritage, the National Film and Television Archive, a Division of the British Film Institute, has compiled a list of 360 key films in the history of the cinema. The long-term goal of the Archive is to build a collection of perfect showprints of these films, which will then be screened regularly at the Museum of the Moving Image in London in a year-round repertory.

BFI Film Classics is a series of books commissioned to stand alongside these titles. Authors, including film critics and scholars, film-makers, novelists, historians and those distinguished in the arts, have been invited to write on a film of their choice, drawn from the Archive's list. Each volume presents the author's own insights into the chosen film, together with a brief production history and a detailed filmography, notes and bibliography. The numerous illustrations have been specially made from the Archive's own prints.

With new titles published each year, the BFI Film Classics series will rapidly grow into an authoritative and highly readable guide to the great films of world cinema.

Could scarcely be improved upon … informative, intelligent, jargon-free companions.
The Observer

Cannily but elegantly packaged BFI Classics will make for a neat addition to the most discerning shelves.
New Statesman & Society

Boris Karloff (the Monster) takes tea

BFI FILM
CLASSICS

BRIDE OF FRANKENSTEIN

. . . .

Alberto Manguel

BRITISH FILM INSTITUTE

bfi

BFI PUBLISHING

First published in 1997 by the
BRITISH FILM INSTITUTE
21 Stephen Street, London W1P 2LN

The British Film Institute exists
to promote appreciation, enjoyment, protection and
development of moving image culture in and throughout the
whole of the United Kingdom.
Its activities include the National Film and
Television Archive; the National Film Theatre;
the Museum of the Moving Image;
the London Film Festival; the production and
distribution of film and video; funding and support for
regional activities; Library and Information Services;
Stills, Posters and Designs; Research;
Publishing and Education; and the monthly
Sight and Sound magazine.

British Library Cataloguing-in-Publication Data
A catalogue record for this book is available from the British Library

ISBN 0–85170–608–8

Designed by
Andrew Barron & Collis Clements Associates

Typesetting by
D R Bungay Associates, Burghfield, Berks.

Printed in Great Britain

CONTENTS

For Rupert, true son of his father,
whose humour he understands, most of the time,
with much love – always.

To have seen this film when one was a child,
in 1935 when it first appeared, is one of the privileges
of being no longer young.
Leonard Wolf

MEETING THE MONSTER
. . . .

I met the Monster was I was ten years old, in 1958, in Buenos Aires. That was the year I was granted the privilege of wearing long trousers and, almost as important, I and a couple of friends were allowed to attend, unaccompanied by an adult, the afternoon-long Sunday shows at our neighbourhood theatre, the Cabildo. Everything about these Sunday shows was generous. The theatre itself seemed to us the height of luxury, its interior a 1930s version of a vaguely rococo Italian palazzo, with gilt mouldings, old plush red seats that smelled of urine on the main floor and newly upholstered vinyl seats that smelled of bleach in the mezzanine, a heavy wine-coloured velvet curtain framing the stage, and six suspiciously Oriental caryatids that made us titter lasciviously because, above their green and gold girdles, the olive-skinned beauties showed their tits. For a few prehistoric pesos you could buy a ticket that allowed you to sit through a live opening act, several shorts and three full-length films, and still have enough change to buy either an Aero bar, made of equal parts of chocolate and air, like a miniature Gruyère cheese, or a box of Sugus, chewy fruit-flavoured caramels of which the best were the red (strawberry) and the worst the green (toothpaste-tasting mint). We stamped our feet demanding that the safety curtain, covered in advertising for local shops, be lifted; we booed and hooted at the miserable pianist who had come to perform for us Offenbach's *Barcarolle*; we laughed uproariously during the cartoons or the Chaplin sketches; and then we settled down for serious business. Listed that first afternoon was a Frankenstein trilogy: *Frankenstein*, *Bride of Frankenstein* and *Abbot and Costello Meet Frankenstein*. We had never seen a Frankenstein movie before but, as if it were a Platonic archetype, the knowledge of what Frankenstein was (in Boris Karloff's definitive incarnation) seemed rooted within us. We were ready to be afraid.

What preparation did we have for fear? None. The gloomy landscapes on the screen were as distantly Mittel-Europa as Hollywood could make them, far removed from our pseudo-Parisian city. Night, the Monster's stalking-time, with its wild howling storms and banging shutters, was never ours – at least in our memory – as if the weather of childhood were protected from high winds. The terror in those films was properly alien, as constructive terror should be, quickening our pulse with a presence that was awe-inspiring and, in the Romantic sense of the word, sublime. It is unfortunate that the word 'horror' was chosen over 'terror' to define the genre meant to explore the dark side of the imagination. In a classic distinction between terror and horror, Ann Radcliffe, the author of *The Mysteries of Udolpho* (1794), noted that terror and horror are of opposite characters since one dilates the soul and sharpens all our faculties, while the other contracts them, freezes them and somehow extinguishes them. 'Neither Shakespeare nor Milton in their fictions, nor Mr Burke in his reflections, never sought in pure horror a source for the sublime, while recognising that terror was one of the highest causes of the sublime; where then is that important difference between terror and horror except that the latter is accompanied by a feeling of obscure incertitude towards the feared evil?'[1] '"Horror"', said Boris Karloff, the Monster himself, 'connotes loathing and revulsion. I prefer the term "terror".'[2]

The word 'monster' – from *moneo*, 'to warn', or *monstro*, 'to show'– seems to imply that monsters hold up a sign that says in large letters, 'Here thou shalt not come'. Since society must define itself by that which it excludes, every social definition carries implicitly – or explicitly – the definition of its reverse. Normality requires abnormality, common bonds circumscribe the notion of the alien, appropriate behaviour reflects the inverted mirror of unacceptability. The conventional image of our social being is surrounded by pariahs, foreigners, freaks. It isn't surprising that monsters have lurked outside our city gates since the oldest vestiges of literature. A Babylonian text from 2800 BC divides monsters into three classes: monsters by excess (giants), monsters by default (such as dwarfs or limbless creatures), and double monsters (Siamese twins). While the birth of a monster of the second and third classes could bode either good or ill, depending on circumstances, a monster born in the first class always signified misfortune.[3] In European folklore, from Ulysses' Polyphemus to the giant in Grimm, the monster is a creature who acts instinctually, a brute easily tricked, whose size doesn't lend him the regal qualities of other large beasts. Frankenstein's Monster is the paradigm of this excess: not only are his bodily parts enormous and his entire form that of a giant, but he himself is an exaggerated result of human creative powers, the product of an imagination bursting across its borders, beyond all social limits, into the margins of that which has been banished and is therefore forbidden.

In an essay on 'The Body of Frankenstein's Monster', Cecil Helman remarked on the curious reciprocity, noted by anthropologists and historians, between the images of our personal body and those of the body politic. For Helman, the society that produced Frankenstein (either Shelley's early nineteenth-century England or Whale's America and Europe of the 1930s) is 'a purely male society, violent and inarticulate, that emerges against a background of feudalism and peasant life. It is a collage of ancient elements, gathered from different pasts, and sutured together within the same body politic. It is animated by science, and by electricity, but it has the brain of a criminal.'[4] Yes, but the metaphoric richness of the Monster's image is far vaster. It embraces a technocratic society of body implants and genetic miracles, as well as their precursors, the satanic mills and the laws of Malthus, but it also reflects the no-man's land beyond society's borders, a land for which we have no vocabulary and whose geography we only dimly recognise in dreams.

Perhaps, vaguely, this was something of what we felt, ten years old and sitting in the adult theatre: that beyond the limits set to us by parents and teachers, beyond acceptable behaviour and the laws of everyday life, was something else, tacitly forbidden and therefore tempting, unspeakable and therefore terrifying, larger than life and twice as natural.

THE MAKING OF THE BRIDE
. . . .

The Universal Film Manufacturing Company was founded in 1912 by Carl Laemmle Sr, a German Jewish immigrant who had come to America in 1884. In 1915, Universal City was erected on a 230-acre ranch in the San Fernando Valley. Universal quickly developed a reputation for the horror genre, a genre it created almost single-handedly. In just over a decade, Universal produced *The Hunchback of Notre Dame* (1923) and *The Phantom of the Opera* (1925), both with the startling Lon Chaney; *The Cat and the Canary* (1927), a haunting spine-tingler with Laura La Plante; *Dracula* (1931), with Bela Lugosi; *The Mummy* (1932), starring Boris Karloff; *The Invisible Man* (1933), with Claude Rains; *The Black Cat* (1934), also with Karloff – and, of course, the *Frankenstein* saga. Several of these classics were filmed under the supervision of Laemmle's nephew, Carl Laemmle Jr, who was made head of production in 1929.

But by 1935, in spite of the successes of the previous decade, Universal found itself in tight financial straits and Laemmle Jr announced that he would produce only seven pictures that year, beginning with what he felt would be a sure-fire success: *The Return of Frankenstein*. At first, Laemmle Jr wanted the German director Kurt Neumann for the film, but James Whale, who was then directing *The Invisible Man* and who had made such a huge money-maker for Universal with *Frankenstein*, said he wanted to make the film himself. Laemmle agreed.

Whale had achieved celebrity as a stage director, first in London's West End and then on Broadway with R. C. Sherriff's grim war play *Journey's End*. As a result, Howard Hughes brought him to Hollywood to work on the dialogue sequences of Hughes's war-in-the-air epic, *Hell's Angels* (1930), first planned as a silent film and later transformed into a talkie. Though the collaboration was not a success (the flying sequences were spectacular but the dialogue scenes were appalling), Whale went on to direct for Universal a rather stilted film version of Sherriff's play, and then the triumphant *Frankenstein* of 1931.

By the end of 1935 the Laemmles were forced to sell their studio. Under the new regime Whale created a finely crafted *Show Boat* (1936) with Paul Robeson, Irene Dunne and Helen Morgan, but that was to be his last success. His next film, *The Road Back* (1937), intended as a sequel to *All Quiet on the Western Front*, about German soldiers returning home to disillusionment and despair, was butchered by censors eager not to offend Hitler's government, and Whale moved on to MGM and then Columbia where he was given shabby, uninspiring scripts. His health began to fail in 1956 and a mistaken diagnosis resulted in an unnecessary electric shock treatment that left him incapacitated. Unable to read, to paint (he had always been a competent artist) or to drive a car, on 29 May 1957 Whale wrote a note addressed 'To All I Love', walked to the shallow end of his pool and threw himself in, head first. In spite of rumours that hinted at murder, the autopsy pronounced Whale dead by accidental drowning.[5]

Whale appears to have been a man who protected his privacy: in Hollywood, though he lived an openly gay life with his lover, actor David Lewis, he rarely gave interviews and never appeared on camera. Publicly, he seemed effete and snobbish. Elsa Lanchester found him 'bitter' and 'nasty'; and he was always derogatory about Karloff, dismissing him with 'Oh, he was a truck driver'.[6] This supercilious attitude may have derived from Whale's peculiar sense of humour. After serving as a young man in the British army at the Somme, Arras and Ypres, he returned to civil life with a strong distaste for authority of any kind, and a keen sense of the absurd, the outrageous and the camp. Christopher Isherwood, in 1954, first outlined the camp sensibility which Susan Sontag later defined as 'love of the unnatural: of artifice and exaggeration':[7] this perfectly describes much of Whale's best work. According to his biographer, James Curtis, Whale's output can be divided into 'jobs' and 'projects'. Jobs were his bread-and-butter films, taken on to fulfil contractual obligations. His projects, on the other hand, were the films he chose to do himself; they were mainly the ones he directed during his years at Universal and they were the ones for which he was to be remembered.

Though it seemed obvious that *Frankenstein* was doomed to return for an encore, *Bride of Frankenstein* was never in Whale's mind a true sequel. It picks up where *Frankenstein* left off, but it is an entirely different creation, both in mood and in style. *Frankenstein* is tragic; *Bride of Frankenstein* both pathetic and grotesquely comic. *Frankenstein* is set in a real (or wishfully real) location. *Bride of Frankenstein* is explicitly Mary Shelley's story, an imagination or a nightmare, a forbidden version of the author herself, marrying the creature she had created.

Whale chose the actors for *Bride of Frankenstein* long before the script was finished. All the main characters were British – a feature the publicity department exploited by having the cast photographed endlessly drinking tea. Karloff as the Monster was of course a necessity. Colin Clive – whom Whale had engaged in 1929 to play the lead in the stage production of *Journey's End*, when Clive was virtually unknown, and who had played the original Dr Frankenstein – would once again play the Monster's maker. Valerie Hobson, under contract to Universal from England, was to portray the other bride, that of Dr Frankenstein. The Bride herself would be played by Elsa Lanchester, who was also to portray Mary Shelley. But to bring to light the undertone of camp humour he was aiming for, Whale specifically brought in two actors: Una O'Connor and Ernest Thesiger.

Una O'Connor (born Agnes Teresa McGlade) was an Irish actress who had made her way to Hollywood in the late 20s. She had played an unforgettable Mrs Gummidge in Cukor's *David Copperfield*, as well as the bristly Mrs Hall in Whale's *Invisible Man*, where her haunting, bird-like figure constantly hovered between horror and slapstick.

Whale had met Ernest Thesiger in England, in a Christmas production in Manchester of *The Merry Wives of Windsor*. 'His appearance,' wrote the Canadian novelist Timothy Findley, who knew Thesiger when he was himself an actor,

> had the same effect as a music cue. Often, what happened was sinister. For instance, if it was a 'costume film', the minute Ernest turned up, you knew the hero was about to be caught in a diabolical trap. Whereas, if the setting was contemporary, the presence of Ernest Thesiger signalled comic complications. He was rarely sinister in modern dress – and I've no idea what that meant, except to say it must have had to do with his physical appearance. Robes and ruffles gave him somewhere to hide – a business suit could not begin to hide him. Hidden, he could be frightening, but revealed, he caused a riot. Ernest Thesiger was a provocateur – in life as well as his career.[8]

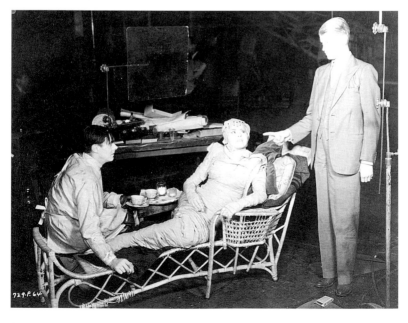

1 2   James Whale (right) with Elsa Lanchester and Colin Clive

When asked his impressions of World War I (in which he had been severely wounded), his answer was: 'The noise, my dear. And the people ...'

The script proved the greatest problem. Before Whale, Mary Shelley's Monster had appeared three times on screen. He was first seen in 1910, in *Frankenstein*, an Edison production directed by J. Searle Dowley and featuring Charles Ogle; five years later, he was reborn in *Life Without Soul*, produced by Ocean Studios and directed by Joseph W. Smiley, with Percy Darrell Standing in the role of the Monster; his third reincarnation was in Italy, played by Umberto Guaracino in an Albertini production, *Il Mostro di Frankenstein*, directed by Eugenio Testa. None of these films was memorable, and Whale felt, rightly, that he had achieved in his version that rarest of things, an original moment of terror. He also knew that he would not be able to recreate what three years of enthusiastic audiences had by now transformed into a foreseeable thrill.

The first treatments were unusable. Scriptwriter L. G. Blechman had Dr Frankenstein and his Elizabeth change their name to Heinrich, pretend to be puppeteers and run off with a travelling circus. The Monster, who hasn't died in the final fires of *Frankenstein*, catches up with them and demands a bride, which the doctor hastily assembles in a caravan hooked up to high-tension cable. The new creature does not survive and the Monster is mauled to death by a circus lion. The treatment by novelist Philip MacDonald was even more preposterous: it proposed a contemporary setting in which Dr Frankenstein tries to sell a death-ray machine to the League of Nations – an apparatus that revives the Monster and in the end destroys it.

William Hurlbut, a Broadway playwright, and John L. Balderston (who had adapted *Frankenstein* for the stage in 1931) collaborated on the first full script of *Bride of Frankenstein*. Balderston's stage adaptation, based on the original novel, had included an attempt to create a female monster. His script (Hurlbut, it seems, had little to do with the actual writing) called for a she-monster made from body parts collected after a train crash, onto which the ingenious doctor stitches the head of 'a hydrocephalic circus giantess who had committed suicide in a fit of sexual despondency'.[9] Ultimately, all that was left of Balderston's script was the prologue featuring Byron, Shelley and Mary Shelley. Hurlbut, in close consultation with Whale, rewrote the entire story (including a few scenes based on another early treatment by scriptwriter Tom Reed). The film took forty-six working days to shoot and ran more than $100,000 over budget, costing approximately $400,000.

According to the picture's editor, Ted Kent – whom Whale had contracted to work on the comedy *By Candlelight* a few months before *Bride of Frankenstein* – Whale

> never entered the cutting room, but we would have a screening at night every week or so for discussion. His scenes would start out simply enough – he didn't like to get things all jumbled-up at once – and then we would build them as we went. He would say, 'That two-shot plays too long. I think we'd better use some close-ups there', and it would get more complex. By the time a scene was finished with, there was very little film left in the can; he would have used every angle he had shot. He prided himself on using it all – he didn't waste a thing.[10]

Whale liked his scripts kept very simple, and much of the actual editing was done on paper, with close-ups clearly indicated between the dialogue.

Whatever Whale's intentions, the script had still to pass through the threatening hands of the censors. *Frankenstein* had not suffered from the censor's scissors when it was released in 1931: though several states did cut various scenes without consulting Universal, the federal censors didn't demand any trimming, not even of the famous drowning of the little girl, until the film's re-release in 1937. *Bride of Frankenstein* was not to share the same fate. By 1934, the power of a number of church-based grass-roots organisations, led by the Catholic League of Decency, forced the Motion Picture Producers and Distributors Association (MPPDA) to set up the Production Code Administration and place it under the direction of the militant Catholic journalist Joseph Breen. Breen immediately objected to the implicit blasphemy in the film's camp humour: 'Throughout the script there are a number of references to Frankenstein [...] which compare him to God and which compare his creation of the monster to God's creation of Man. All such references should be deleted.'[11]

Other deletions included a scene in which the Monster witnesses a couple exchanging love vows, cut 'to avoid the obvious inference that the monster is watching a physical affair between the two people', and the use of the word 'mate', which Breen found offensive. A few months later, Whale sent Breen a changed script, but Breen still wasn't satisfied and sent a new list of 'suggested' deletions. Not only did Whale follow Breen's new recommendations, he even suggested that Breen had forgotten some of his earlier objections. On 10 December 1934, Whale wrote to the Administration:

> Dear Mr Breen,
> Herewith are the proposed changes, which deal with your letter of Dec 5th, and also your letter of December 7th. As, however, the former letter is fuller, I think it best to send on the letter I had written immediately after the conference, as in your letter of December 5th there are several points about God, entrails, immortality and mermaids which you did not bring up again, and I am very anxious to have the script meet with your approval in every detail before shooting it.
>
> All best wishes,
> Yours sincerely,
> James Whale[12]

Whatever other changes may have been, God, entrails, immortality and mermaids remained in the final cut of *Bride of Frankenstein*, which presumably met with Mr Breen's approval.

In the end, America was not alone in its objections. Trinidad rejected the film simply because 'it is a horror picture'; so did Palestine and Hungary. China, Singapore and Japan made important deletions, and Sweden's were so numerous that the film was almost released as a short.

Against these odds, it is extraordinary how much Whale was able to preserve from his original conception. Fundamentally, in spite of the graftings and amputations, *Bride of Frankenstein* is as close to Whale's imagination as he might have hoped for: terrifying, subversive, hilariously irreverent and yet touched with rare dignity and pathos.

MARY TELLS A STORY

Though Universal's publicity department advertised the film as *The Bride of Frankenstein* in posters, press releases and theatre lights, the article does not appear when the title comes up at the beginning of the film itself. Immediately following, over ominous music by Franz Waxman[13] and rings of rising smoke, we read: 'Suggested by the original story written in 1816 by Mary Wollstonecraft Shelley.' Through Hollywood's reliance on the classic reference for decorous support, the year is given, the time is set.

A furious storm ('weird howling, thunder rolling and the sound of violins', reads the script) over Lake Geneva. High on the cliffs, a house and, at the window, a young man in Romantic garb, looking out into the darkness. This is aristocracy, depicted in a style that eclectically sums up the clichés of wealth (what the script calls 'sentimentally luxurious'): large gilded mirrors, plush furniture, a huge fireplace. A uniformed maid crosses the room, led by three Afghan hounds on a leash.

Three people are in the room: two men – the one at the window, another one writing – and a young woman, doing needlework. Graham Greene once said that he detested historical films in which, speaking down to the audience, one character conversing with another points at a third and says: 'See him over there? The world will hear much about him, mark my words! His name is Wolfgang Amadeus Mozart!' Whale avoids these gauche introductions by cramming the names of the three

1 6   Mary Shelley (Elsa Lanchester), Byron (Gavin Gordon), Shelley (Douglas Walton)

characters into the first two-minute speech, each line receiving a cut of its own. (Breen had demanded the deletion of much of the dialogue 'in which the three characters boast of their infidelity, immorality, and adultery'.) Smoking a cheroot and rolling his r's, the man at the window wonders whether 'an irate Jehovah' is pointing his arrows directly at the unbowed head of England's greatest sinner, 'George Gordon, Lord Byron'. Or are they meant for England's greatest poet, 'our dear Shelley'? 'What of my Mary?' asks the fey Shelley. 'She is an angel,' Byron answers. Mary, in a dress embroidered with iridescent sequins and dragging a seven-foot-long train (a dress that took seventeen Mexican seamstresses twelve weeks to make), looks up from her woman's work. Cut, following the censor's demands, was a shot 'in which the breasts of the character of Mrs Shelley' were 'exposed and accentuated'[14] by the fabulous dress. Mary Shelley does indeed look angelic.

This angel, however, has created Frankenstein: 'a monster made of cadavers out of rifled graves', Byron explains – thereby endorsing the common metonymy that confuses the creator with his creation, lending the Monster his father's name. (Later, in the film's climax, Dr Pretorius will make the same mistake and pronounce the female creature 'the Bride

'Mary Shelley does indeed look angelic'

of Frankenstein' when in fact she is the Bride of the Monster. Unless, of course, Pretorius means 'the Bride belonging to Frankenstein' …)

Byron is in charge of the recapitulation. By and large we, the audience that has come to see the film, have seen the earlier *Frankenstein*. We are acquainted with the story, we recognise the Monster. We come like the audiences of ancient Greece to a further episode in a plot we know well; we are attending a part of a ritual in which only the tone, the details of this particular chapter, the slant of the telling will be new to us. Byron's flashbacks are a reminder that we are on familiar ground, in a common nightmare that we thought had ended. 'But that was not the end of the story,' Mary says. And the film proper begins.

When *Frankenstein* opened in 1931, the Quebec censor board – one of the strongest in North America – had objected to its Faustian theme. T. B. Fithian of Universal showed a preview version to a couple of Catholic priests in Los Angeles and, to calm their fears, suggested that the picture could be set within a narrative frame that would temper any hint of blasphemy 'through the agency of a suitable foreword or some preface that would indicate the picture was a dream. Perhaps we could open it on the book with the off-scene voices of Shelley and Byron and Mrs Shelley discussing a fantastic tale and dissolve into the picture.' The board relented, and in the end *Frankenstein* was shown as Whale had wished. But Whale didn't forget Fithian's suggestion and, a few years later, made use of it to tell the story of the Monster's Bride. *Frankenstein* had no supporting narrative frame; the opening credits appear over a vague and evil face with whirling eyes, after which the nightmarish events unfold sequentially. *Bride of Frankenstein*, on the other hand, exists explicitly as a fiction, as a tale told in Mary Shelley's voice.

Wetted by Byron's flashback, we find ourselves at the end of the first *Frankenstein*, among the ruins of the burning mill. The camera dollies over the curious crowd, as the servant woman Minnie (Una O'Connor), in a vaguely Mittel-European costume, sends out her first howl. The Burgomaster (E. E. Clive) pompously orders everyone home. The Monster has disappeared in the fire; Henry Frankenstein lies apparently lifeless in the debris and the villagers depart to take his body back to his bride-to-be.

The parents of Maria – the little girl the Monster had unwittingly drowned – stay on among the smouldering ruins, hoping to find proof that their child's murderer is dead. 'If I can see his blackened bones, I can sleep at night,' says the old man to his wife. As he speaks, the floor beneath him crumbles and he falls into the millpond. His wife faints.

Waxman's swelling music announces the appearance of the Monster. The camera, travelling carefully along the blazing water, focuses on the Monster's face appearing from behind a sunken timber. This, like the face of Garbo, is one of the icons of our time. Garbo's face, with its disturbing classic features, is the face of Dante's Beatrice, the 'radiant visage that receives our soulful longings', the reflection of that part of ourselves which we associate with spiritual beauty and transcendental wisdom. ('Think of nothing', director Rouben Mamoulian is said to have instructed Garbo when she asked him for direction in the unforgettable final shot of *Queen Christina*. That vacuum was made for us to lose ourselves in.) The Monster's face is its counterpart, its shadow, the face of our subhuman self, bearing the features we fear will one day emerge from a distracted mirror – the face in Dorian Gray's picture, the face of the wicked Mr Hyde. If Garbo's face is divinely empty, the Monster's face is demonically full, bursting at its visible seams with that which we wish to conceal. It is not 'evil' (just as Garbo's is not 'good') but execrable (as Garbo's is immaculate). It is,

'It is a perfect failure of a face'

more than that of any other humanoid monster, a face dreamed up by someone who knows what a face should be but cannot quite manage to recreate it, a mistaken face, a face so big that it grips us with the fear that if we were to come close to it (in Chesterton's words) 'the face would be too big to be possible'. It is a perfect failure of a face, a mock version of the biblical description of a face created 'in His own image'.

Whale had famously chosen Karloff, whom he had seen in the gangster film *Graft* (1931), as the actor was sitting in the Universal cafeteria having lunch.[15] (Another version has it that David Lewis suggested Karloff for the role. According to Lewis, Whale's response was 'Boris who?') Born in England, Karloff had reached Hollywood via Canada and gained recognition as a powerful actor for his playing of the killer-convict in Columbia's *The Criminal Code* (1931). Karloff's natural face seemed to Whale monstrously perfect as a basis for that of the Monster. Whale, who had some talent as an artist, made drawings of Karloff's head, adding 'sharp, bony ridges where I imagined the skull might have been joined'.[16] 'We had to surmise,' Karloff explained, 'that brain after brain had been tried on that poor skull, inserted and taken out again. That is why we built up the forehead to convey the impression of demoniacal surgery. Then we found the eyes were too bright, seemed too understanding, where dumb bewilderment was so essential. So I waxed my eyes to make them heavy, half-seeing.'

Following Whale's sketches (though he never acknowledged the inspiration) make-up artist Jack P. Pierce was in the end responsible for the monster's appearance. Pierce had achieved a reputation as an inventive genius after creating Conrad Veidt's horrible grin in *The Man Who Laughs* (1929). Preliminary sketches by other Universal make-up artists show monsters who look like aliens, wild men or robots. Whale and Pierce agreed that the Monster had to have a pitiful humanity. 'I made him the way textbooks said he should look,' Pierce recalled in 1939.[17]

I didn't depend on imagination. In 1931, before I did a bit of designing, I spent three months of research in anatomy, surgery, medicine, criminal history, criminology, ancient and modern burial customs, and electrodynamics. My anatomical studies taught me that there are six ways a surgeon can cut the skull in order to take out or put in a brain. I figured that Frankenstein, who was a scientist but no practising surgeon, would take the simplest surgical way. He would cut the top of the skull off straight across like a potlid, hinge it, pop the brain in, and then clamp it on tight. That is the reason I decided to make the Monster's head square and flat like a shoe box and dig that big scar across his forehead with the metal clamps holding it together.

The notion of the lid-like skull-top, however, was not Pierce's invention; it is described in the script as being 'like the lid of a box'. Nor were the two puzzling metal studs sticking out at the side of the Monster's neck Pierce's idea: they were designed by Universal's poster illustrator Karoly Grosz in his 1931 sketch of a robot-like monster. Pierce credited himself with the invention: he explained later that he'd intended these studs to be 'inlets for electricity – plugs such as we use for

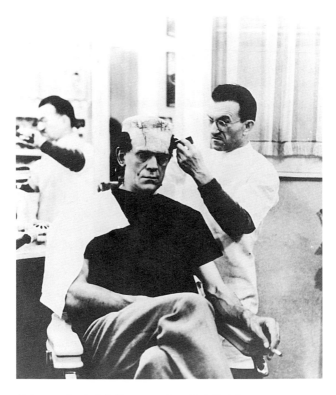

Make-up artist Jack P. Pierce at work on Boris Karloff

lamps or flatirons. Remember, the Monster is an electrical gadget. Lightning is his life force.' Finally, Pierce covered Karloff's face with blue-green greasepaint, which photographed grey. The make-up took six hours every day.[18]

The Monster drowns the old man. This is not a haphazard death: this is deliberate murder, bred by revenge. In this beginning, the Monster is not a victim but a creature of revenge, striking back when hunted, goaded into violence and responding to horror with horror. He embodies the fate of the outsider, reflecting back the image society projects on him.

Next, the Monster drowns the old woman by throwing her into the pit. The owl, creature of witches and night, looks on. (The owl replaced the rat which the censors demanded be removed, 'as its portrayal has in the past proved offensive'; this lent a darker, more subtle, less repulsive touch to the scene.)

Whale said he wanted *Bride of Frankenstein* to be a 'hoot'. Now, after the first double murder, the Monster meets Minnie. The old couple had uttered terrible, dramatic screams; Minnie's are too shrill to be terrifying – an artifice, an exaggeration. Una O'Connor had made this piercing, whooping sound her trademark, a touch of camp *avant la lettre*. Minnie's comic scream has here a similar effect to the knocking at the gate in *Macbeth*. According to Thomas De Quincey, who commented on the porter's scene in a well-known essay, the disruption, the grotesque note that exaggerates the sound of pathos so that it becomes funny, taking us 'into the region of human things', happens so that our sympathy goes for a moment to the murderer: 'a sympathy of comprehension, a sympathy by which we enter into his feelings, and are made to understand them'.[19] Minnie's scream allows us to shift from the viewpoint of the Monster's victims to that of the Monster himself.

The body of Henry Frankenstein is brought to his bride in a grey, melancholy procession leading up to the castle gates. Elizabeth (Valerie Hobson) rushes to meet them, wanting to know what has happened to her bridegroom. 'How can we tell you, Milady?' says one of the townspeople, while a close-up shows a townswoman (played by David Lewis's sister, whom Whale tried to help in those difficult Depression days) obligingly blinking back tears. Once again, the drama is undercut by grotesque comedy: Minnie arrives at full speed, screeching her awful news that the Monster is alive. But no one pays attention to what appears to be more of Minnie's hysterics. 'Nobody believes me,' she says indignantly. 'Right, I wash my hands of it. Let them all be murdered in their beds!' Minnie is a comic Cassandra.

Inside the castle's great hall, Henry's body lies inanimate on a table. We are reminded of the moment of the Monster's birth in *Frankenstein*, except that here the creator is usurping the place of his creature. This fundamental theme – the identification of the creator with the creation and vice versa – is drawn out by Whale throughout the film: Mary Shelley and the Bride played by the same actress, the Monster demanding a mate when Dr Frankenstein marries Elizabeth; the Monster taking Frankenstein's place by kidnapping his maker's mate.

The parallel is stressed in Minnie's next scream as she sees the doctor's hand move. 'He's alive!' she shrieks. This line had been the catchphrase in *Frankenstein*, uttered by the doctor in mad glee at the creation of his Monster and thereafter pasted across billboards throughout the moviegoing world. The same phrase will be picked up, once again, in the second act of creation, when the Bride is brought to life, but what is here coloured by Minnie's camp tone will later, in the mouth of the doctor, become ghoulish, even prurient. In all three cases of the

Elizabeth (Valerie Hobson) in the room where she is nursing Henry

dead coming to life – the Monster in *Frankenstein*, the doctor in this scene, the Bride in the film's climax – it is the right hand, traditionally connected to the heart, that first flickers with vital energy.

Elizabeth nurses Henry in a room with crisscrossed latticed lights – lights that, in John Mescall's dramatic photography, destroy any illusion of convalescent serenity. Henry raves, wanting to forget the ugly events of the past, but quickly passes from repentance to ambition: 'The power to create a man!' he exclaims, eyes wide with feverish excitement. Elizabeth, terrified, answers cautiously: 'We are not meant to know these things. It's the devil that prompts you.' As Henry denies the evil of what he has done, his nightmare becomes Elizabeth's: she suddenly sees, there in the room, the threatening appearance of 'a figure like death'. When Henry tells her there's nothing there, she collapses in a faint.

Of all the characters in *Bride of Frankenstein*, Colin Clive as Dr Frankenstein is the most wooden, carrying a single expression throughout the film which apparently served him to denote everything from exultation to paralysing fear (made worse by a fall that ripped the ligaments of his knees and forced him to play many of his scenes sitting down or leaning on crutches for his close-ups). Fortunately, Dr Frankenstein is, in the Whale saga, merely a secondary figure to set off the action, and it is a wonderful paradox that while Clive's performance is stilted, Karloff, stiff with padding and make-up, gives here what is arguably the best, most complex performance of his career. The story escapes the title character: it belongs to the resurrected Monster, to his brief but unforgettable Bride and to the villainous Dr Pretorius.

THE DOCTOR AND THE DEVIL

A banging at the front door. Thesiger's entrance, as Dr Pretorius, is formidable, mirroring the 'figure like death' of Elizabeth's hallucination. In the next shot his angular face dominates the screen, wickedly menacing. Minnie repeats his name over and over again, as if she hadn't heard it correctly or as if she were not able to retain it. 'There's no such name,' she mutters to herself. Seven times the name Pretorius is spoken in the course of the next few seconds. There exists a tradition from the late Middle Ages that in order for the devil to remain in human company his name must be repeated at least three times (as in Goethe's *Faust*); this triple call will stand as an invitation ('Talk of the Devil and he's bound to appear'[20]). God's name cannot or must not be uttered; the devil's name, on the other hand, must be pronounced out loud both to retain him and to order him to go. The devilish Pretorius has now been introduced by name to the world of sinners, and in their world he will remain.

For Mary Shelley, the subtext of her *Frankenstein* was Milton. The epigraph of the novel is from *Paradise Lost* ('Did I request thee, Maker, from my clay/ To mould me man? Did I solicit thee/ From darkness to promote me?'); the Monster's account of his own creation is paraphrased from Milton's description of Adam's awakening in Eden; the Monster follows the example of Milton's Satan ('Evil thenceforth became my good'); among the books which the Monster reads in the cottage near Geneva is a translation of *Paradise Lost* (the cottagers are of course French Swiss). For Whale, the film's story is upheld by the sixteenth-century legend of Faust, consolidated by Marlowe and by Goethe. Henry Frankenstein's ambition and his search for forbidden knowledge echo those of Dr Faustus; Pretorius, in Thesiger's unsettling incarnation, is a nineteenth-century Mephistopheles.

Dr Pretorius (Ernest Thesiger), 'wickedly menacing'

Pretorius blackmails Henry, telling him he's responsible for the Monster's crimes, and insists that they work together, 'not like master and student, but as fellow scientists'. (In Goethe's *Faust*, Mephistopheles also agrees to collaborate with the doctor: '*Here* I'll work for you and heed your every whim; when we meet again *over there*, you can do the same for me'.[21] Goethe lends his Mephistopheles the same kind of ironic nastiness that Thesiger gives Pretorius.) Pretorius then reveals that he too has created life and wants Henry to see his experiments 'in his humble abode'. Henry is tempted. 'Is it far?' he asks. 'No, but you will need a coat,' adds Pretorius with dubious solicitude.

In his laboratory (the steps to which are out of *Dr Caligari*, by then an icon of science gone mad) Pretorius proposes a toast of gin – 'my only weakness', he says, as he will later say of the cigars he will offer the Monster. 'To a new world of gods and monsters.' Henry nervously refuses to drink.

Pretorius brings out a coffin-like box. Inside the box are six glass jars, each one containing a tiny figure Pretorius has grown 'from seed'. The figures are a queen, a Henry VIII-like king[22] (madly in love with the queen), a scowling archbishop, a devil who looks like Pretorius himself

Pretorius with the tiny devil figure

('Or do I flatter myself?' he asks), a ballerina who only dances to Mendelssohn's 'Spring Song' and a languorous mermaid. (Cut from the final release was a seventh figure, a baby, played by midget actor Billy Barty and, according to the script, intended to resemble a miniature Boris Karloff.) Pretorius's figures are assigned a role according to their congenital characteristics. For instance, its beauty suggested that the first figure be a queen; a disapproving look made the third one an archbishop.[23]

It seems extraordinary that, while agreeing to the censor's cuts, Whale was able to retain intact the character of the Mephistophelian Pretorius. Apparently lost on the MPPDA was the double entendre of the word 'seed' and the demonic nature of Pretorius. Considering his devil in the jar, Pretorius suggests that it might be amusing if we were all devils – 'and no nonsense about angels and being good'. As befits Mephistopheles, Pretorius tempts Henry with the Scriptures. 'Male and female created He them,' he reminds his pupil and suggests they populate the earth with a man-made race. Henry is appalled but Pretorius is relentless. Alone, he reminds him, Henry created a man. Together, they will create his mate. 'You mean…?' asks Henry, aghast. 'Yes, a woman,' concludes Pretorius. 'That should be really interesting.'

In Mary Shelley's novel, it is the Monster himself who makes this demand of his creator. 'I am alone, and miserable; man will not associate with me; but one as deformed and horrible as myself would not deny herself to me. My companion must be of the same species, and have the same defects. This being you must create.'[24] In Whale's version, it is not the Monster's demand but Pretorius's ambition that becomes the motive behind the Bride's creation. The new world will be born not out of the need for love but out of the lust for power. Pretorius will later convince the Monster of this 'need', but the true reason is that, like a shadow God, Pretorius wants to populate the earth with his own handicraft.

THE MONSTER SPEAKS!

In contrast with Pretorius's fearful place, we now follow the Monster into a bucolic setting. In these contrasts Whale is at his best. The 'normal' humans in the unnatural laboratory counterpoint the 'abnormal' Monster in the midst of bountiful Nature. Without forcing the issue, Whale points to a contradiction which allows us, once again, to feel sympathy for the 'deviant', the Monster. Like a poor animal, he eats something that looks like a carrot (he is vegetarian, thank the stars!); then he bends over to drink in an idyllic pool. Suddenly, as he drinks, he sees his own image in the water; like Caliban, he is horrified at his own face and tries to destroy it by beating the water with his hands. In Mary Shelley's novel, the scene echoes the moment in *Paradise Lost* when Eve sees herself for the first time reflected in the water of a pool – except that in Eve's case, the startling image pleases her and she returns to it.[25] There is a very moving paradox in the fact that the Monster reacts to his face much as other people do: he is suffering the outsider's fate, that of seeing himself with the hater's eyes. But he is also recognising, beneath the bestial traits, the possibility of evil violence.

Suddenly, in the idealised setting – pine trees, painted sky, mountains, sheep – the Monster sees a beautiful human creature, a young shepherdess. The 'sacrificial innocence' of this scene is accentuated by a cut to a bleating lamb (but who is the innocent victim? The shepherdess? the Monster?). Always striving for beauty, the Monster tries to reach her; seeing him, she screams and falls into the water. (Death or near death by water is a constant theme in Whale, as it was for Mary Shelley, mirroring to us, after the facts, Shelley's death in the Gulf of Spezia four years after *Frankenstein* was published and Whale's death in his swimming pool in 1957.) The Monster, who, after throwing little Maria into the lake in the previous film, has learned his lesson – that human bodies drown – nobly rescues the sinking shepherdess. But her screaming doesn't stop. Two hunters hear her and shoot at the Monster. Like a wounded animal, he escapes through the forest.

The villagers are incensed and rush off to tell the Burgomaster that the Monster is indeed alive. Officiously, the Burgomaster decides to send the men and dogs on the Monster's trail, and orders that the women be locked up for their safety. 'Monster indeed!' he grumbles superciliously. 'I'll show him!' Like Minnie's appearances, the Burgomaster scenes serve to pull the audience away from sheer terror into uneasy irony (we know that the foolish man will *not* show the Monster anything), without ever allowing us to relax into straight comedy. The audience's laughter never lasts long during *Bride of Frankenstein*. Once, when Whale was watching the film at a local theatre and chuckling audibly, a woman in front turned round and snarled at him: 'If you don't like the show, you can damn well leave!'[26]

Top The Monster sees his reflexion in the water
Bottom The Monster rescues the shepherdess from drowning

The chase begins, through the woods and under a menacing sky. Now the idyllic landscape is a place of pain and a setting for injustice (since we know that the Monster meant no harm). Men and dogs pursue him. In a beautiful close-up, lit from the left, the Monster's face becomes young, frightened, almost angelic: it is one of Karloff's most touching scenes. The face of evil possibilities has become a face of possible goodness.

The villagers trap him high on a rock (Whale may have had in mind one of those paintings of hunted stags dear to Victorian parlours: Karloff's hands are raised like antlers while the hounds bay underneath). The Monster lifts a rock and lets it fall on his pursuers, but they succeed in overpowering him. They put him in chains, tie him to a pole and raise him up in the air like a wounded Christ on the cross (a bold shot in view of the censor's vigilance). The Christ imagery is stressed by the villagers jeering and mocking the captured monster.

The Monster is taken to prison and strapped, the huge chains are hammered down. Two policemen are left to guard him, but the chains don't hold him for long. He pulls them out, rushes to the door and, as one of the policemen shoots at him, escapes into the streets. Ironically, the

'The Monster's face becomes young, frightened, almost angelic'

camera cuts to the Burgomaster telling the people: 'Go to your homes, quite harmless.'

The Monster's escape creates mayhem in the town. 'Where is Frieda?' asks a desperate mother as a crowd of virgin-like girls, veiled in white, move slowly towards her. (Who are these vestal adolescents? Are they coming from school? From church? From some expiatory Christian rite?) But we know that Frieda is no more. The distraught mother discovers Frieda (or rather Frieda's feet) by a roadside cross. A couple of villagers, Herr and Frau Neuman, are the next victims. The Monster is on a killing frenzy.

At this point a scene was cut in which the pedantic Burgomaster, after dismissing the townspeople as 'superstitious infidels', is pulled through the window and beaten to death; the cut was probably made by the censors on the grounds that the scene undermined the triumph of rightful authority. The Burgomaster's murder was replaced by another scene which, because it was shot after the film had been finished, lacks Waxman's supportive music. We see a gypsy camp at night. Another worried mother. Another disparaging man, her husband. Sitting by the fire, an unpleasant grandmother grumbles about the lack of pepper and

Tied to a pole, 'like a wounded Christ on the cross'

salt for the roast (the little things we care about in moments of mortal danger!). The Monster arrives, attracted no doubt by the smell of food, and the women run off in panic. The husband tries to defend the camp but the Monster hurls him to one side and digs into the fire for the food, thereby learning another lesson: fire burns. Clutching his scorched hand (he also has a bullet in his arm), the Monster runs away again into the forest.

Mary Shelley subtitled her novel 'The Modern Prometheus', a myth that, together with Milton's Satan, much appealed to the Romantic spirit as an icon of revolt against tyranny both human and divine. According to Theogones, Prometheus was the Titan who created the first man and woman out of clay, and then stole fire from heaven for the sake of his creation. For Mary Shelley, Prometheus is Dr Frankenstein; in Whale's mythology, he is also the fire-stealing Monster. The use of fire, which the Monster needs for warmth and food, is a learned craft which, like everything else in the human world, the Monster must acquire through suffering.

The learning begins with water and fire and continues with air, with music. The Monster arrives at a hermit's cottage, lost in the woods, where he hears a violin playing Schubert's 'Ave Maria'. (Anachronism is not an error in Whale's film. Peter Conrad has pointed out that a story told in 1816 can include a melody composed in 1825, and later, the body of a woman who died in 1899, in order to assert its universality.[27] The story of Frankenstein, like that of Prometheus, like that of Faust, happens in every country and in every age.) 'Music soothes the savage breast': the cliché becomes a powerful scene of respite, putting a momentary end to the Monster's hounding, and the cottage is shown almost as an antonymous image of both Frankenstein's luxurious castle and Pretorius's evil laboratory. This is a moment of pathos: the Monster is now a child who has run away from his abusive parents.

The hermit, also an outsider (he is poor, he is blind), is the first person to be kind to the Monster – because he can't see him – and welcomes him into his home. In Shelley's novel, the Monster (who by then has learned to speak) makes his entrance with the words 'Pardon this intrusion'. 'This sentence,' comments Leonard Wolf, 'is the most superbly realized literary achievement in the whole of *Frankenstein*. To savour the tact that informs Mary Shelley's choice of phrasing here one must pause for a moment to remember what an elaborate structure of pain and self-loathing the creature's autobiography has by now become. This meeting of the visibly appalling with the blind is stunningly imagined and made graceful by the language of diffidence and courtesy in which it is couched. As an epigraph (or an epitaph) for humanity, 'Pardon my intrusion' is unsurpassed.'[28] Whale, obviously conscious that these words would prove absurdly comic in the Monster's mouth (had the script provided him with an opportunity to learn to speak), replaced the introduction with a series of grunts which Karloff delivered with magnificent conviction.

'If you understand me, put your hand on my shoulder,' says the hermit. The Monster obeys; he cannot speak but he can understand. This raises in the finicky viewer an ancient question: how is language learned? For centuries, Europe debated the possibility of a primordial and universal language, not acquired but inbred and spoken by Adam in Paradise. To discover what that language was, King Frederick II placed a couple of new-born babies in the care of remote shepherds whom he instructed never to speak to the children while at the same time paying close attention to the first words they might utter. The experiment was unsuccessful because the babies died soon afterwards,[29] but the conviction that language was a gift we were born with remained unscathed. The Monster obviously knows what words mean, as Frederick imagined his babies knew – in the same way that he has a natural understanding of morals and moral behaviour, a sense of beauty and of justice: what he must acquire (often against this innate knowledge) are the conventions of his society, the modes and manners of social behaviour, the vocabulary of social language. The notion implicit in both Mary Shelley's novel and in Whale's two chapters of the Frankenstein saga is that language is inherent to us, that it is part of our human constitution – not an acquired talent, but a function of the brain. What we learn are the sounds that stand for the meaning, but the Platonic forms of our primordial memories carry language and its craft within us from before birth. The Monster holds within his cobbled brain the possibility of lofty moral dialogue and a penchant for Schubert.

The hermit and the Monster suit one another. It is a fair exchange: 'I will look after you and you will comfort me,' he says, echoing Lear and his restored Cordelia. 'Perhaps you are afflicted too.' And finally, 'We shall be friends.' No doubt Whale, as a gay man, must have relished the double entendre in this scene. ('I wonder if he means *friend*,' asks

Vanessa Redgrave in *Prick Up Your Ears*.) There is something tacitly but strongly erotic here: the meeting of the two men, both outcast, both unwanted, who find they can share house under a common bond – all this underlined by the Monster patting the hermit on the shoulder with his magnificent large hand, while a tear rolls down his scarred left cheek. A crucifix (a reminder that Christ urged us to love our fellow men, and suffered for it) glows in the background, lit while the scene grows dark.

The hermit's lessons progress quietly, as he teaches the Monster at the dinner table. Like the posters announcing 'Garbo Speaks!' to promote the diva's first incursion into the talkies in *Anna Christie* (1930), the pre-publicity for *Bride of Frankenstein* included the banner 'The Monster Speaks!', and a contest was launched asking the public to guess what Karloff's first words were going to be. Not many must have guessed the correct answer. In response to the hermit's prompting, the first word we hear the Monster utter is 'bread'.

After 'bread' the Monster learns 'wine' (the Christian vocabulary continues), and then 'friends', that ambiguous word which the Monster has already heard but still finds hard to believe. 'Wine is good, friends is good,' he learns. And then, a cigar. The Monster recoils from the lit

3 4   The Monster puffing on his cigar

match, afraid of the flame – the roasting gypsy fire has burnt his hand and, in the first *Frankenstein*, fire is sent to destroy him – but he must learn that good can come of it. Laughingly, the hermit shows his new room-mate how to smoke. The Monster puffs at the cigar while the hermit plays the violin. All is peace and domestic bliss. 'Alone, bad. Friend, good,' says the Monster. He has learned the basis of social behaviour.

The Monster's speech remains problematic. In Mary Shelley's novel the Monster can write eloquently in florid nineteenth-century English prose the calvary of his autobiography. On film, such eloquence would only seem grotesque.

> 'Man knows that there are in the soul tints more bewildering, more numberless, and more nameless than the colours of an autumn forest,' wrote G. K. Chesterton. 'Yet he seriously believes that these things can every one of them, in all their tones and semi-tones, in all their blends and unions, be accurately represented by an arbitrary system of grunts and squeals. He believes that an ordinary civilised stockbroker can really produce out of his own inside noises which denote all the mysteries of memory and all the agonies of desire.'[30]

Beyond the grunts and squeals, a speaking Monster presented a puzzling challenge for Karloff. In *Frankenstein*, he had succeeded brilliantly in creating a convincingly moving character for the creature through soft or angry looks and through a series of rasping sounds. 'I had to portray a sub-human of little intelligence and without speech, still getting over the sympathetic qualities of the role. When the monster did speak, I knew that this was eventually going to destroy the character.' It didn't. In *Bride of Frankenstein*, Karloff managed to convey, through the halting speech and the broken words of the Monster, an even stronger sense of mistreated innocence than in *Frankenstein*, and a plea for understanding that demanded from its audience both sympathy and compassion.

The scene at the cottage allowed Mel Brooks, forty years later, one of the most successfully parodic moments in *Young Frankenstein* (1974), Brooks's brilliant spoof of the Frankenstein saga. In Brooks's version, the blind hermit (Gene Hackman) scalds the Monster (played with Karloffian gusto by Peter Boyle) with hot soup and then is unable to fill his guest's mug with wine which he splashes all over the table. The Monster is left hungry and thirsty in spite of the hermit's good intentions, which is what eventually happens, on a larger scale, in Whale's version. In spite of the hermit's kindness, society will not allow a monster to be happy (the reflection of an experience which Whale, as a gay man in the 1930s, could hardly have failed to understand).

Once again, the two ubiquitous hunters arrive. Seeing the Monster, they bluntly reveal the truth about the stranger to the astonished hermit. 'He isn't human. Frankenstein made him out of dead bodies.' The Monster tries to save himself and, in the ensuing fight, the cottage is set on fire. The hunters lead the hermit away. Left alone like a frightened child, the Monster comes out of the smoking cottage wailing 'Friend!' In the shadow of a sideroad crucifix (again, the Monster is compared to the persecuted divinity), he frightens a group of children as he lumbers along. The moment of respite is gone. Pathos gives way to terror.

The cemetery at night. Fog. The Monster comes across a statue of a bishop or saint. Whale had wanted the Monster to come upon an image of Christ on the Cross to remind us that the Monster (like Christ

Mel Brooks' *Young Frankenstein:* the scene with the hermit

Himself) has met the other, the ugly face of 'Christian' charity. There exists a powerful design by art director Charles D. Halls of the Monster tugging at the loincloth of a crucified Christ, while a statue of hollow-eyed Death stands large in the foreground – but the censors intervened.

The town's search party approaches and the Monster hides in an open grave. In the background looms yet another cross. The townspeople pass by. Inside the tomb, the Monster discovers a sarcophagus with a woman's beautiful face carved on the lid. 'Friend,' he calls to her, passing one of his gigantic hands over the stone features (the British censors had this scene cut because of its necrophiliac undertone). The stone is silent.

Pretorius arrives with two assistants. Standing over a tomb, presumably nearsighted, he orders: 'Read the inscription. What does it say?' 'Died 1899, Madeleine Ernestine, beloved daughter of...,' mutters one of the assistants. 'Oh, never mind that,' says the callous Pretorius. 'How old was she?' 'Nineteen years and three months.' The youth of the woman suits the doctor and his assistants set themselves to work. Now Pretorius takes off his coat and becomes the archetypical mad scientist, rubbing his hands as he stands expectantly in his white uniform. 'Pretty

The Monster descending into the grave

little thing, in her way,' says one of the three (a moment of bad synch because none of them move their lips). Then Pretorius adds ghoulishly: 'I hope her bones are firm.'

The assistants leave Pretorius behind. 'I rather like the place,' he chuckles as he sets out his dinner of wine and roast chicken on the lid of the sarcophagus, decorated – *memento mori* – with a skull. 'I give you the Monster,' he says, and cackles with laughter. This is Thesiger at his best, hardly having to move in order to convey a malevolent detachment, a crazed egotism.

The Monster appears from a shadowy corner. Pretorius reacts with no surprise and even offers him a cigar. Just as the hermit's cottage held an inverted mirror to the evil of Pretorius's place, the offer of a smoke mirrors malignantly the hermit's kind gesture (from the days before cancer warnings). Pretorius and the hermit are like the good and evil angels of our Adam-like Monster: the hermit blind to superficial appearances, Pretorius incapable of perceiving the human core.

Pretorius tells the Monster his plan of creating a woman for him, a 'friend', and explains that he must be used to put pressure on Dr Frankenstein. 'I know him,' says the Monster, acknowledging his creator.

'Made me from dead. I love dead. Hate living.' Then the Monster looks at the skull and muses, Hamlet-like, on this reminder of mortality. His, however, is not a meditation on death as the end but on death as the beginning, as the source.[31] From the dead he was made, among the dead he will find his companion, to the dead he will return. To the ancient question, 'Can these bones live?', the Monster answers yes in three words: 'Woman. Friend. Wife.' The Monster has learned much since the hermit taught him his first vocabulary.

TWO BRIDES FOR TWO BROTHERS

Back in the castle, where Henry and Elizabeth are busily packing to leave, Minnie announces that Dr Pretorius has returned. Once again, Pretorius comes between the bridegroom and his bride, physically standing in the way of 'sanctified' marriage and excluding the woman from the society of men. Henry orders Minnie to send him away, but mysteriously Pretorius appears through a back entrance (by now his diabolical capabilities are no longer questioned by the audience) and with unctuous irony offers Henry and Elizabeth congratulations on their marriage. Elizabeth tells him his visit is 'most unwelcome' and lets him know that they're not afraid of him. Nevertheless, she exits, leaving Henry with Pretorius, her husband in the hands of Mephistopheles, as if realising the impossibility of struggling against the doctor's spell. Pretorius calmly explains to Henry that everything is set and that he has secured 'a perfect human brain, already living but dormant'. When Henry once again refuses, Pretorius calls in the Monster. 'He's quite harmless,' he says mockingly as Karloff staggers in and Henry recoils in terror. 'Except when crossed.'

The Monster then pronounces, for the first time, his maker's name, 'Frankenstein'. This is an important moment, the creature naming the god who made him, acknowledging the existence of the force that gave him life. In Judaeo-Christian religion pronunciation of God's name in vain is forbidden by the third commandment. For that reason, the unpronounceable name of God (the Tetragrammaton) is written in consonants only, and usually substituted by the word *Adonai* meaning Lord. Uttering a god's name is a challenge to his powers since, if the god is truly a god, the sound itself will annihilate the speaker. With the

Top The Monster as voyeur

Bottom The Monster outside the window in the earlier *Frankenstein* (1931)

utterance of the name Frankenstein, the Monster places himself and his maker in the same human and absurd realm.

Since Henry still won't agree to collaborate with Pretorius, the Monster, following Pretorius's orders, goes and stands outside Elizabeth's window. Here is the classic scene of the Monster as voyeur, a scene repeated endlessly through generations of horror films – King Kong watching Fay Wray, Dracula peering into the women's bedroom, the Golem stalking the young girl, Dr Caligari's somnambulist following his victim, even the Monster outside Mae Clarke's window in Karloff's first *Frankenstein*. Here we, the viewers, are forced to become accomplices in the intrusion, our eyes taking the Monster's place outside the forbidden chamber as we become the voyeurs of the voyeur. Like the Monster seeing his reflection in the pool, we see ourselves for what we truly are.

Inside, Minnie is uneasy about leaving her mistress alone but, since Elizabeth insists that all will be right, she reluctantly obeys. The Monster enters the room and the audience finds itself, once again, in the realm of pure terror. For a moment, Elizabeth thinks the intruder is Henry; then she sees the monster and screams. As he drags her across the room to the bed (the censors let this one pass) she screams out her husband's name, not only as a cry for help but also as an implicit accusation, since Henry is of course the Monster's maker. It is as if in shouting out 'Henry!' she were naming her own husband in the shape of the monster he had imagined. In that shout, the Monster becomes the person of her husband whose bestial nature (by a slip of the tongue) Elizabeth has recognised.

Terror turns once again to camp when Minnie tells everyone that Elizabeth has been kidnapped by the Monster. Pretorius prevents Henry from sending out a search party and guarantees her safe return.

The Monster carries Elizabeth up a craggy mountain, malignant clouds blackening the background. Nature is no longer the idyllic setting into which the Monster first escaped. Like the Monster itself, Nature has learned to be evil, full of jagged edges and eerie shadows. The Monster drops Elizabeth inside a gloomy cave, a violent contrast to her elegant bedroom. In Frankenstein's castle the promise of sex was refined, socially tamed, acceptable; here, the viewer knows, it must be brutal, unconventional, unrestrained. Monstrosity and the erotic often share a common territory of exclusion: dwarfs and giants become pornographic icons, black sexual prowess is cited as a racist commonplace, the sensuality of the Jews was conjured up in anti-Semitic tracts. (In *Young Frankenstein*, Mel Brooks made the Monster's sexuality explicit, when Madeleine Kahn as Elizabeth suddenly becomes aware that *all* the body parts of a monster are gigantic, and bursts into a rendition of 'Oh mystery of life, I now have found you!')

Henry returns defeated to the lab, the place where the Monster was first created, where new scientific machinery has been added since those early experimental days. As Pretorius chortles that once they would have been 'burnt at the stake as wizards for this experiment', Henry begins to work on a heart. 'I will make him greedy for the dust,' says Goethe's Mephistopheles;[32] Whale's Mephistopheles offers his Faust the same temptation, and mutters soothingly: 'The human heart is more complex than any other part of the body.' But the scientific magic breaks down and the heart's beatings stop. 'This heart is useless,' groans Henry. 'I must have another. And it must be sound. And young.'

One of the ghastly assistants (whose name was changed from Fritz to Karl during the shooting) is sent to the Accident Hospital for 'a female victim of sudden death'. For a thousand crowns, Karl has agreed to run

4 2   Pretorius and Henry at the operating table

this errand, but instead of resorting to the hospital's morgue he lurks in a dark street, waiting. The scene ends just as a young woman approaches.

Back in the lab, Henry suspects that the heart may not have come from the hospital, but Pretorius dismisses his doubts and urges him on. Now the line between body-snatching crime and the mortal sin of murder has irredeemably been crossed: no longer is Henry merely working to bring dust to life; he has become an accomplice to turning living flesh to dust. In Kenneth Branagh's 1994 version (called *Mary Shelley's Frankenstein* to stamp it with a seal of authenticity) the Monster rips out Elizabeth's heart, allowing her body to be used to create the monstrous Bride; the idea is effective, but the bloody depiction is a good example of horror superseding terror, and one watches the surgical butchery not with fear (as provoked by Karl's lurking) but with revulsion.

Exhausted, Henry falls asleep; the Monster wakes him, ordering him to continue. To keep the over-anxious Monster out of the way, Pretorius gives him a sleeping drug. Since Henry wants proof that Elizabeth is still alive, Pretorius has him speak to her on a primitive telephone ('this electrical machine') held by the wicked Karl. But just as she's about to tell him her whereabouts, Karl covers her mouth and drags her away.

The creation of the Bride is an extraordinary sequence, even more skilfully shot by cinematographer John J. Mescall than that of the Monster's creation in *Frankenstein*. The special effects department of Universal had invented, at Whale's bidding, a number of meaningless instruments that clicked and spun and crackled to supplement the apparatus of the first film. Mescall, who worked best when drunk, photographed the gadget-filled laboratory and the fantastical operation from all sorts of lopsided angles which, in Ted Kent's editing, become a mounting puzzle of tortured images building up to the Bride's birth.

Heart and brain are ready; the operating table looms on one angle, the instrument table on another. Henry picks up the beating heart with a pair of pincers, just as Karl comes in to announce that the storm is rising. A bandaged head is all that can be seen of the body on the table. Pretorius, for whom science is merely a tool to prove his own creative greatness, rhapsodises on the marvel that 'lying here, in this skull, is an artificially developed human brain'.

'Are the kites ready?' asks Henry. (The North American public would know about Benjamin Franklin's experiment and grasp the inference: electricity from the heavens, 'irate Jehovah's arrows', will give the new being life.) Electrodes are placed on the creature's head while upstairs wild bonfires rage, the kites are pulled back and the 'cosmic diffuser' (whatever that might be) is lowered. It's a wonderful scene, cutting from the feverish activity of the doctors to the electric arches reflected in the metal circles of the machinery.

The upwards shot reveals the inside of the tower, copied from Piranesi's famous *Prisons* engravings. The cables are sent down and Henry climbs to the roof to send off the kites – fantastic origami contraptions that will capture 'the spark of life'. Now the table with the body rises into the sparkling and fuming heights and out onto the terrace in the storm. While the wires buzz and crackle in the night, the faces of Henry and his teacher are diabolically illuminated.

The Monster has woken and climbs laboriously to the top of the tower. A frightened Karl tries to ward him off with a burning torch but the Monster, no longer afraid of fire, picks him up and hauls him over the wall. In the meantime, lightning has struck one of the kites and Henry,

Cinematographer John J. Mescall with Boris Karloff

grinning with pleasure and conceit, again lowers the body. Waxman's music strikes a symphonic crescendo.

The 'cosmic diffuser' is lifted, the bands that hold the body to the table are detached, and Pretorius and Henry inspect their handicraft. The camera closes in on the bandaged hand and slowly, like a larva stirring in its cocoon, the fingers of the new creature's right hand begin to move. The bandaged mouth makes a muffled sound. Carefully, anxiously, as we hold our breath, the two doctors remove the bandage from the creature's eyes. The close-up focuses on the eyes: the pupils dilate, the creature can see. 'She's alive!' exclaims Henry. 'Alive!' – repeating the cry of creation. Hastily, they unfasten yet more bands and straighten the table, forcing the creature to stand. Like a cataleptic patient (or rather like Karloff in his stiffest performance, in Karl Freund's 1932 Egyptian horror story *The Mummy*), the creature raises both her arms, as if to sleepwalk. Then she lowers them again and her head droops down in a faint.

The next scene is the most famous one in the film, and certainly one of the all-time glories of horror films. Here Whale manages to elicit both terror and pathos by means of a camp rendition of the ceremonies

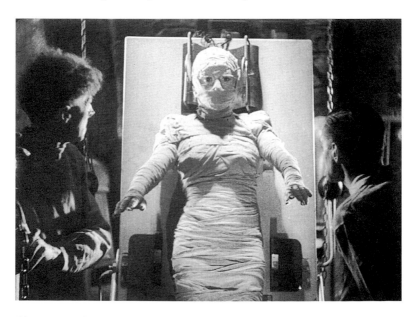

'The creature raises both her arms'

of birth and marriage. Standing between Pretorius and Henry, the female creature is clothed in all her splendour, half Nefertiti,[33] half ghost with her long white bridal gown, or death robe, or swaddling cloth, her arms still bandaged (by the studio nurse), her face carrying Elsa Lanchester's cute pouty look, her eyes unblinkingly wide open, her cheeks crossed with scars, her hair unforgettably coiffed with streaks of white lightning, she stands halfway between a zombie and a future punk, outlandishly sexy. ('Doesn't Elsa have the most beautiful shell-like ears?' Charles Laughton asked Whale at the preview.) The Bride's hair was a complicated construction. Four tiny tight braids were made to stand at the top of Lanchester's head, and on these was anchored a wired horsehair cage about five inches high. Lanchester's own hair was brushed over this structure and the two white hairpieces were applied over the lot.

As the close-ups quickly succeed one another, we see her head from several angles, luminous against the black background: left, right, upwards. 'The Bride of Frankenstein!' announces Pretorius proudly. As in a grotesque wedding march, the Bride struts stiffly forward. Her uneasy steps harshly choreographed – broken, falling back – she is held

by her two creators as she begins to move. Then she lets go of them and stands alone – funny, grotesque, hideous, impossibly exaggerated, terrifying, independent.

The Monster sees her. Now he has the same young face he had as a pitiful, hunted animal, Adam seeing Eve for the first time. 'Friend,' he says tenderly. Slowly, the Bride turns her head, emits a hideous squawk and, as he touches her arm, screams. This scream is in effect the story's conclusion, the last act beyond which the tragedy is allowed no other outcome. If she, the Monster's equal, the one and only being who might understand that his patched-up looks hide a sensitive, almost human soul, recoils in horror, what can the Monster expect from the rest of the world?

According to Lanchester, the Bride's screams were inspired by the sound made by the swans of London's Regent's Park, which she and Charles Laughton enjoyed watching. 'They're really very nasty creatures, always hissing at you,' she recalled. 'So I used the memory of that hiss. The sound-men, in one or two cases, ran the hisses and screams backwards to add to the strangeness. I spent so much time screaming that I lost my voice and I couldn't speak for days.'[34] (Madeleine Kahn turned the Bride's hiss into a mating-call in *Young Frankenstein*.)

Henry leads her away. As the Monster tries once again to approach her, Pretorius interferes but is pushed to one side. Relentlessly, walking to the fate he knows awaits him, the Monster goes to her. With Waxman's haunting music in the background, the Monster takes the hand of his Bride-to-be and smilingly caresses her bandaged fingers. As he leans towards her, as if to kiss her, she screams again, falling back into Henry's arms. The Monster is devastated, a jilted lover. 'She hates me. Like others,' he says, and in a fury of dejection he begins to destroy the lab that created them both, the birthplace of his sufferings.

'The lever!' shouts Henry as a warning. 'You'll blow us all to atoms!' explains Pretorius. The Monster eyes the destructive lever just as Elizabeth, who has somehow managed to escape her prison, reaches the laboratory tower. 'Henry,' she calls from outside, drawing the Monster's attention as she tries to open the door. Henry rushes to her but refuses to escape with her. 'I can't leave them, I can't,' says Henry, suddenly guilt-stricken, suddenly conscious that he is responsible for his ill-begotten children. 'Yes,' orders the Monster, with more generosity and understanding than Henry could ever hope to have. 'Go. You live.' And turning to the evil Pretorius, he speaks his final sentence: 'You stay. We belong Death.' With those words, he reaches for the fatal lever. The Bride hisses a hideous swan-from-hell hiss. The lever descends, the lab explodes, the tower shakes, timbers fall, walls collapse. Destruction seems total.

The poet Edward Field concluded his own version of the story with these words:

> Perhaps somehow the Baron got out of that wreckage of his
>   dreams
> with his evil intact if not his good looks
> and more wicked than ever went on with his thrilling career.
>
> And perhaps even the monster lived
> to roam the earth, his desire still ungratified,
> and lovers out walking in shadowy and deserted places
> will see his shape loom over them, their doom –
> and children sleeping in their beds
> will wake up in the dark night screaming
> as his hideous body grabs them.[35]

'Destruction seems total'

That is the real ending. The film's coda is barely noticeable. Oblivious, we see Henry and Elizabeth run to the side of a hill and, against a sky of rising clouds, embrace. 'Darling, darling…' says Henry, patting her head soothingly. Over their faces appear the unnecessary words THE END.

VIEWS OF THE BRIDE

In the May 1935 issue of *Fantasy* magazine, Forrest Ackerman, who had been invited to the preview of *Bride of Frankenstein* by a generous publicist, wrote a rapturous account of the film. The article credits Ed Thomas as co-author, but Ackerman claims that he alone saw the film with 'more than a quarter of an hour footage than was projected upon general release.'[36] Though most of the review is little more than a summing-up of the plot, Ackerman acknowledged that the film was even better than *Frankenstein*. 'The story,' he noted, 'instead of inspiring horror, as the former did, awakens the deepest compassion for the Monster. Karloff makes him lovable and engaging, his helpless exploits as a murderer entirely excusable.' *Hollywood Reporter*, previewing films for the market, declared *Bride of Frankenstein* 'one of the finest productions that has come off the Universal lot for many a day. Mounted extravagantly, gorgeously photographed, excellently cast. … Exhibitors can guarantee a fine production of a creep yarn, beautifully acted and directed.' And *Variety* called it 'an imaginative and outstanding film'.[37] In the mainstream American press, reaction was unanimously favourable. The usually censorious Frank S. Nugent in the *New York Times* called it 'a first-rate horror film… Mr Karloff is so splendid in the role that all one can say is "he is the Monster".'[38] In New York and Los Angeles, *Bride of Frankenstein* was a huge box-office favourite. At the Pantages Theatre on Hollywood Boulevard, which could seat almost 3,000 people, it was shown eleven times a day.

In Britain, in spite of its popular success, there were doubts about the film's artistic merits. Though *Kinematograph Weekly* called it a 'spectacular thriller, a macabre morality play',[39] not everyone agreed. 'Poor harmless Mary Shelley,' began a review in the *Spectator*:

> when she dreamed that she was watched by pale, yellow, speculative eyes between the curtains of her bed, set in motion a

vast machinery of actors, of sound systems and trick shots and yes-men. It rolls on indefinitely, that first dream and the first elaboration of it in her novel, *Frankenstein*, gathering silliness and solemnity as it goes; presently, I have no doubt, it will be colour-shot and televised; later in the Brave New World to become a smelly.[40] But the one genuine moment of horror, when Mrs Shelley saw the yellow eyes, vanished long ago; and there is nothing in *The* [sic] *Bride of Frankenstein* at the Tivoli to scare a child.

This is not Mrs Shelley's dream, but the dream of a committee of film executives who wanted to go one better than Mrs Shelley and let Frankenstein create a second monster from the churchyard refuse, a woman this time, forgetting that the horror of the first creation is quite lost when it is repeated, and that the breeding of monsters can become no more exciting than the breeding of poultry. ... This is a pompous, badly acted film, full of absurd anachronisms and inconsistencies. It owes its one moment of excitement less to its director than to the strange electric beauty of Miss Elsa Lanchester as Frankenstein's second monster. Her scared vivid face, like the salamander of Mr De La Mare's poem,[41] her bush of hardly human hair, might really have been created by means of the storm-swept kites and the lightning flash.

The review was by Graham Greene.[42]

CREATION MYTHS: LIGHT AND DUST

The myth of Frankenstein casts its hideous shadow over vast libraries of Western literature and film, so that H. G. Wells's Dr Moreau and the unfortunate scientist of *The Fly*, the Tin Man of *Oz* and the artificial humans in *Bladerunner*, the dreamed man in Borges's 'The Circular Ruins' and the misnamed and nightmarish Terminator all share the same mythical realm. In its various transformations, Frankenstein rejoins a much earlier myth: that of Adam the knowledge-seeker who, like Prometheus, dares to undertake that which God has forbidden. The serpent's hissed vow to Eve – 'You shall be as gods' – is twofold. It promises the light of knowledge, the divine fire from Olympus; and also the supreme gift of breathing life into dust, of creating as only God

Himself is able to create. Before the gates to this power, God has set an angel with a flaming sword because, as every artist understands, God, with sublime egotism, wants to be the one and only Creator.

Among Dr Frankenstein's most celebrated ancestors are the magi of Jewish folklore. According to kabbalistic tradition, the golem (a word meaning 'incomplete substance') is a creature made out of clay and lent life by the application of certain letters that spell out either the secret name of God or the Hebrew word for truth. Psalm 139, in words that could have been spoken by Mary Shelley's Monster, reads: 'My substance was not hid from thee, when I was made in secret, and curiously wrought in the lowest parts of the earth. Thine eyes did see my substance, yet being unperfect [golem]; and in thy book all my members were written, which in continuance were fashioned, when as yet there was none of them.' Several medieval legends tell the story of just such a creation. The earliest one, preserved in the *Sanhedrin*, says that the scholar Rava created a man and sent him to Rabbi Zera. Rabbi Zera spoke to it but the creature didn't answer. 'Are you made by one of the companions?' the rabbi said at last. 'Then return to your dust.' The creature obliged. The most famous of these legends, which served as the basis for Gustav Mayrink's novel *The Golem* (1915) and for the film five years later, tells the story of the sixteenth-century Rabbi Löw ben Bezulel of Prague who created a clay servant to help out in the synagogue and brought it to life by writing on its forehead the word *emet* (truth). Establishing a tradition that later man-made monsters would follow, the creation turns wild and threatens to destroy its creator. The Rabbi undoes the magic by removing the first letter of the word *emet*, so that now it spells *met* (death).[43]

Creating from male 'seed' creatures in his own image (as Pretorius does in his glass jars), with no need for a woman (as Dr Frankenstein realises), is the alchemist's method, the patriarchal dream, the mad scientist's goal. From the Jewish golems to the animated sculptures of fable and science – Eve created out of Adam's rib, Pygmalion's ivory woman, Collodi's Pinocchio, the eighteenth and early nineteenth-century automata that so enchanted Mary Shelley's circle, Dr Pretorius's homunculi – men have imagined themselves capable of creating life without women, depriving women of the exclusivity of the power to conceive. No women take part in Henry Frankenstein's creation of the Monster, or later in that of the Bride: it is an affair conducted only among men. For the medieval kabbalists, this attempt at conception without male-female coupling was a supreme sin. According to the sixteenth-century Spanish scholar, Rabbi Moisés Cordovero, 'the union and coupling of man and woman is a sign of coupling from on high',[44] and any diversion from this consecrated method is a denial of the will of God. In attempting to create life from seed or from dead body parts, Dr Frankenstein and his brethren are sinning against God's omnipotence.

There is, however, another side to the myth: the plight of the Monster itself who, like Adam the sufferer, is a piece of living clay that never asked to be brought into this world. At its rawest, most primordial, the creature is the Golem, the puppet granted life, Frankenstein's surgical experiment; at its most exalted it is Hamlet, it is Segismundo in Calderon's play *Life Is a Dream*, wondering whether he isn't a speck of dust bound in a nutshell or merely a shape seen in sleep.

The problems of creation – the problems of the creator and the problems of the creature – can be seen as cinematic problems. Lumière's 'I want to make images move' echoes Dr Frankenstein's 'I want these dead bones to breathe', and bringing light into the darkness (as Prometheus did by stealing the fire) is surely one of the definitions of film itself. Isn't the myth of Frankenstein an essentially cinematographic myth, a metaphor of cinema itself? In both, life is created out of assembled pieces, 'in continuance', edited together in the hope that the result will somehow move – in spite of being many times hampered by a deficient brain. The townspeople cry out against the Monster's evil influence when in fact it is incapable of either good or evil. Its death is proclaimed many times but it continually returns with new vigour. Producers have the ambitions of a Pretorius and directors the anguishes of a Henry Frankenstein, calling out to their creature for 'action'...

It may be that one of the key moments in the history of cinema occurred outside the boundaries of conventional chronology, in a villa on the shore of Lake Geneva, on a famous rainy evening in June 1816, several decades before Monsieur Lumière's invention. After reading a French translation of German ghost stories, Lord Byron suggested to his friends – John Polidori, Claire Clairmont, Shelley and Mary Shelley – that they would each write a tale in imitation of those hauntings. That night, lying in her curtained bed, Mary Shelley had a vision. She saw 'the pale student of unhallowed arts kneeling beside the thing he had put together'. She saw 'the hideous phantasm of a man stretched out ... the horrid thing … looking on him with yellow, watery, but speculative eyes'.[45] She saw, in fact, the birth of the first film monster.

Until Mary Shelley, the monsters of literature either begin their awful careers fully formed, or metamorphose malignantly from something docile into something deadly. Medusas, manticores, ogres, ghouls, bloodthirsty ghosts, demons rarely show their birth certificates; sometimes dead bodies come back to life, but resurrection does not create new beings. Mary Shelley's Monster is neither a ready-made horror nor a nineteenth-century Lazarus: it is an impossible *Gestalt* whose birth we are made to witness, a medley of bits and bobs that somehow, against all odds, can move and breathe – like images on a screen.

The EDISON
KINETOGRAM
VOL. 1   LONDON, APRIL 15, 1910   No. 1

SCENE FROM
FRANKENSTEIN
FILM No. 6604

EDISON FILMS TO BE RELEASED
FROM MAY 11 TO 18 INCLUSIVE

J. Searle Dowley as Frankenstein (1910)

Cinema consists largely in granting movement. Lumière's first experiments are astounding not because of the captured images themselves, but because these images have been captured alive: the first audiences were as terrified at seeing a locomotive enter a station on the wall in front of them as later audiences were at seeing the Monster rise out of the foul waters of the mill. In Mary Shelley's night-time vision, and then on the printed page, the first stirrings of the Monster have a quality that is essentially that of film: not arrested in technical description but unfolding in cinematic time. This quality evolved with the medium itself as movies became more intricate and more elaborate. J. Searle Dowley's clownish Monster of 1910 or Paul Wegener's overbearing Golem of 1920, stiffly inching their way from frame to frame, become in 1979 David Cronenberg's oozing Brood and Ridley Scott's carnivorous Alien, rushing into life and towards the audience. No longer did the Creature rise from under a surgical sheet or from clean dust; it now burst through the very skin of its involuntary creators.

At the same time, the mad scientists also changed their pace. Nowadays they no longer stand to one side of their creation, wringing their hands in glee or anguish. No longer Promethean geniuses of

Paul Wegener's *The Golem* (1920)

ambiguous ambition, the new fashioners of monsters have become helpless subjects in a society that has itself transgressed unspoken limits (sexual genetics or space exploration). In today's world, the updated Dr Frankenstein (as seen for instance in Kenneth Branagh's version) is less of a rebel and more of a victim.

Perhaps there is a third aspect of the myth. Dr Frankenstein may defy the divine prohibition against attempting that which only God can do, but at the end of our century the tale can be turned to show God Himself cast in Dr Frankenstein's role, bringing us, human creatures, to life and then turning away, horrified at His own creation. If He is a god, He is a god defeated, no longer able even to judge His corruptible creatures. He resembles the post-Holocaust God of this Jewish legend:

In some obscure village in central Poland, there was a small synagogue. One night, when making his rounds, the Rabbi entered and saw God sitting in a dark corner. He fell upon his face and cried out: 'Lord God, what art Thou doing here?' God answered him neither in thunder nor out of a whirlwind, but with a small voice: 'I am tired, Rabbi, I am tired unto death.'[46]

ANOTHER BRIDE
STRIPPED BARE BY HER BACHELORS, EVEN

In 1951, Jorge Luis Borges suggested that 'each writer creates his own precursors'.[47] The same can be true of image-makers. After Whale's *Bride of Frankenstein*, after the appearance of the electric Elsa Lanchester, in her streaming and scandalous hair, wedding (or refusing to wed) the inheritor of Adam, the Bride becomes one in a bevy of brides – brides of film, painting, photography and installation art – that, surprised in her light, reflect back several of her terrifying facets.

The Bride is a *femme fatale*. She has been brought into a realm of power-thirsty patriarchs anxious to people the world with their creations. In their eyes, she does not exist for her own sake: she is merely a female counterpart to the Monster — maybe the future mother of a monstrous litter bred by more traditional methods, but primarily a living doll created for the Monster's pleasure. In this world of men, the Bride is damned if she does and damned if she doesn't. Were she to consent to the coupling, she'd be a complacent whore; unwilling to submit to what she is told is her duty, she becomes a reluctant whore, and an instrument of male perdition. Because of her refusal, the jilted Monster brings the drama to its apocalyptic conclusion, choosing to return to his allotted dust, dragging the Bride and Pretorius and the abominable laboratory with him in his fall. In his chosen end, the Monster is proven not guilty. He may have sinned earlier in his tattered life, but now he is willing to mend his ways if only this woman would stand by his side. And stand she won't.

The woman created for the purpose of male pleasure, and whose very existence leads to his downfall, the archetypical Eve, is exemplified by the female robot in Fritz Lang's *Metropolis*. Brigitte Helm, as Maria, has been lying on a table under a glass cover, bound by metal bands, while Rotwang, the evil inventor, transfers her in flesh and spirit to an automaton. After the transformation is complete, Rotwang introduces the Monster-Maria at an aristocratic party, by having her emerge from a wedding cake-like urn in a flowing, luminous dress. Lanchester's Bride raised her arms in front of her to come into the world; Maria lifts hers from her sides and slowly begins to rotate her hips in a seductive,

5 6 *Metropolis* (1925): Rotwang, the inventor, with his creation

hypnotic dance, while the light shows her almost naked body under the dress. In *Bride of Frankenstein*, the deadly sexuality of the new creature is suggested; in *Metropolis* it is explicit. The men at the party turn lustful eyes on the apparition, while the audience knows that in their lust is their doom.

The Bride's blood ties flow forward as well. In Max Ernst's *La Toilette de la mariée* of 1940, the Bride has been given back the censored breasts of Mary Shelley.[48] She is naked, but a gown of red feathers is draped over her shoulders and a huge owl-like headdress lends her the startled and monstrous look of Lanchester's Bride. In a male world, her beautiful feature is her body, the attribute of Aphrodite; her head, her intelligence, symbolised by the owl of Athena, is monstrous, since here learning ill befits a woman. Her male escorts (the mad scientists) have been transformed as well: one is a green crane with a man's legs,

Max Ernst, *La Toilette de la mariée*, 1940. © ADAGP, Paris and DACS, London 1997.
Photograph © 1995 The Solomon R. Guggenheim Foundation.

carrying a wicked lance, suggesting that the Bride requires (as in so many wedding rituals) punishment to prove her future husband's hold over her; the other is female, since men can usurp for their pleasure features allotted to the female identity (the creation of life seen as science, cookery and dress-making as art, child-raising as pedagogy, lesbian relationships as male pornography, finery and adornment as ceremonial accoutrements), and her hair fans out like a bishop's purple cloth. Karl, the bestial assistant, has become the explicit depiction of the situation's ambiguity: a green hermaphrodite dwarf with a penis and four breasts. Alone in the whole group, he senses that something terrible is taking place and he is weeping.

As a sexual partner for the Monster, the Bride must subdue her person and exaggerate instead her monstrously sexual characteristics. Censorship would not permit her the underlinings of a Dietrich or a Mae West, and Whale, Lanchester and Pierce (the responsibility of the choice

Man Ray, Portrait. © Man Ray Trust/ADAGP, Paris and DACS, London 1997.

Photograph Telimage, Paris

was apparently shared) settled on the Bride's hair, since hair is associated with animal nature, with the unruliness of female sexuality.[49] For a woman to shed her erotic qualities – in North African rituals of mourning, in the constant presence of the God of orthodox Judaism, as a punishment for having had sex with the enemy in post-Vichy France, to take on a warring role among the men, like Joan of Arc – her hair must be shorn; to heighten her eroticism, she lets it grow. And long hair disguises the presence of the brain beneath the skin: all surface and no depth, a cascade of hair offers the head to a male beholder as a docile object of sensual pleasure rather than a threatening source of reason and intelligence. The Bride's head is almost all hair.

In Man Ray's solarised photographs of the 1930s, women's hair spreads out to occupy almost the entire space of the frame, so that the face seems attached to the hair rather than the other way round. These heads of female hair are textures, patterns, waves of sand or water. Man Ray apparently hunted for women's faces that allowed him to 'draw with light', and, according to one of his friends, cared little about 'his subject's thoughts, fame or fortune'. These 'deformations', as he called them, 'filtered like hair through a comb of light … dreaming objects that are talking in their sleep.'[50] Talking but asleep, alive and yet dead: the description fits the Bride perfectly. Man Ray's somnolent heads belong to the Bride's sisters, recreated for the eye of a man.

Eight years before Whale started filming *Bride of Frankenstein*, another Bride had made her appearance in America. The French artist Marcel Duchamp finished in 1923 a construction he had begun in 1915 which he titled *The Bride Stripped Bare by Her Bachelors, Even*. It consists of two glass panels (cracked in transit and repaired by Duchamp), each with a strange blue, brown and grey piece of machinery painted on it. An accompanying booklet 'explains' the work and its function. Nothing in the booklet (or for that matter in the work itself) is immediately or clearly identifiable; nothing – neither the parts, nor the machine itself and its disturbing name – can be given a socially acceptable meaning. Duchamp's pseudo-technical vocabulary brings to mind Pretorius's pseudo-scientific euphemisms ('Speak … through this electrical machine') – but, according to Duchamp, 'It wasn't for love of science that I did this; on the contrary, it was rather in order to discredit it.'[51] In the same way, Dr Frankenstein's experiments 'discredit' the humanistic view of proper scientific research. 'The Bride,' wrote

Marcel Duchamp, *The Bride Stripped Bare by Her Bachelors, Even* (The Large Glass) 1915–23. Philadelphia Museum of Art: Bequest of Katherine S. Dreier. © ADAGP, Paris and DACS, London 1997

Duchamp in the booklet, 'accepts this stripping by the bachelors, since she supplies the gasoline to the sparks of this electrical stripping; moreover, she furthers her complete nudity by adding to the first focus of sparks (electrical stripping) the second focus of sparks of the desire-magneto.'[52] Vaguely, the reader-viewer realises that the Bride apparently consents to whatever it is that is being done to her: this barbarous 'scientific' act, this creative 'stripping bare'. Isn't she a *femme fatale* who gets what's coming to her? Or is she an erotic plaything, all body and no brain? (The French call a provocative woman an *'allumeuse'*, one who sparks the flames, and in Branagh's version the Bride, suddenly realising what she is, literally sets herself and the house on fire.)

Whatever the case, in amatory terms the Bride is culpable and the actions of her bachelors appear necessary and justified. This is the key to Rotwang's use of Maria; this is the logic that governs Dr Frankenstein's own experiments. In both cases, the created woman is the guilty device, a sacrificial tool through which an ambitious man (in the patriarchal vocabulary the adjective is one of praise, not one of condemnation) plans to transform or take over his society.

The Bride Stripped Bare By Her Bachelors, Even tempts the viewer with interpretation. Our need to make sense of what we see lends the parts of the construction a kinetic purpose, and our habit of finding language decipherable assumes a message in the name. 'Psychological realities and the realities of art,' says the poet Octavio Paz, 'exist on different levels of meaning'[53] and he suggests that Duchamp's *Bride* can be seen as a version of the myth of the Great Goddess, the Virgin, the Mother, the Exterminator and Giver of Life. 'It is not a modern myth,' says Paz. 'It is the modern version (and vision) of Myth.'

Whale's *Bride* is, apparently, much easier to decipher. At least there is a storyline, a framework, characters that portray emotions, causes and effects. And yet what exactly is the meaning of the strange, man-made Bride, that modern Eve, beyond its sexuality? Who is this monstrous version of the angelic Mary Shelley, this transformation of the delicate Elsa Lanchester? Towards the end of her life, Lanchester complained that the ghost of the Bride pursued her everywhere and that children in grocery stores still recognised her not as herself but as the She-Monster from Dr Frankenstein's laboratory. What symbolic power does that white-streaked, frizzy-haired Bride have, constructed (stripped bare and reassembled) by her Bachelors, the mad doctors and their bestial assistants? She too is, like Duchamp's creation, a modern version (and vision) of Myth, rooted in time and endlessly pregnant with meanings which we create in generation after generation of film viewers. Whale's *Bride* (as Paz said of Duchamp's) is a work 'in search of significance' and therefore inexhaustible.

There are imaginary creatures that somehow don't seem imaginary because the world seems inconceivable without them; they are necessary inventions, like unicorns and dragons, and belong to an inner landscape as grounded in our reality as that of our everyday lives. The Monster and his Bride are part of that imperishable and common fauna.

NOTES

· ·

1 Quoted in *Romantisme noir*, ed. by Liliane Abensour and Françoise Charras (Paris: Cahiers de l'Herne, 1978).

2 Quoted in Scott Allen Nollen, *Boris Karloff: A Critical Account of His Screen, Stage, Radio, Television, and Recording Work* (Jefferson, NC, and London: McFarland and Co., 1991).

3 Leslie Fiedler, *Freaks: Myths and Images of the Secret Self* (New York: Simon & Schuster, 1978).

4 Cecil Helman, 'The Body of Frankenstein's Monster', in *Essays in Myth and Medicine* (New York and London: W. W. Norton & Co., 1991).

5 Kenneth Anger, *Hollywood Babylon II* (New York: Dutton, 1984).

6 Elsa Lanchester, *Elsa Lanchester Herself* (London: Michael Joseph, 1983).

7 Susan Sontag, 'Notes on "Camp"', in *A Susan Sontag Reader* (New York: Vintage, 1983).

8 Timothy Findley, 'Parcel Post', in *Soho Square III*, ed. Alberto Manguel (London: Bloomsbury, 1990).

9 David J. Skal, *The Monster Show: A Cultural History of Horror* (London: Plexus, 1993).

10 Quoted in James Curtis, *James Whale*, (Metuchen, NJ, and London: Scarecrow Press, 1982).

11 Gerald Gardner, *The Censorship Papers: Movie Censorship: Letters from the Hays Office 1934 to 1968* (New York: Dodd, Mead & Co, 1987).

12 Ibid.

13 Waxman's brilliant score for *Bride of Frankenstein* won him a contract as Universal's musical director. Years later, in new arrangements by Charles Previn, it would serve as music for several Universal serials, including *Buck Rogers* and *Flash Gordon*. Waxman went on to write the scores for, among many other films, *Sunset Boulevard* (1950) and *A Place in the Sun* (1951).

14 Quoted in Skal, *The Monster Show*.

15 Peter Underwood, *Karloff* (New York: Drake, 1972).

16 Curtis, *James Whale*.

17 'Oh You Beautiful Monster', *New York Times*, 29 January 1939, quoted in Nollen, *Boris Karloff*.

18 'The make-up is copyrighted by Universal,' Karloff commented in a 1968 interview, 'which is very funny, when you think that the man who did it now sits in a valley in California, retired, and not getting a penny for it.' In Mark Shivas, 'Karloff, Still Eager to Scare Us Witless', *New York Times*, 14 April 1968.

19 Thomas De Quincey, 'On the Knocking on the Gate in *Macbeth*', in John Gross (ed.), *The Oxford Book of Essays* (Oxford and New York: Oxford University Press, 1991).

20 Iona Opie and Moira Tatem (eds.), *A Dictionary of Superstitions* (Oxford and New York: Oxford University Press, 1989).

21 Goethe, *Faust: Der Tragödie erster Teil*, lines 1656–69 (Stuttgart: Reclam, 1986).

22 One of Whale's in-jokes, since Elsa Lanchester's husband, Charles Laughton, had just won an Academy Award for *The Private Life of Henry VIII*.

23 These special effects were achieved through back projection and by using man-sized jars.

24 Mary Shelley, *Frankenstein* (1818 edition) in *The Annotated Frankenstein*, with introduction and notes by Leonard Wolf (New York, 1977).

25 Milton, *Paradise Lost*, Book IV, II, 23–32.

26 Curtis, *James Whale*.

27 Peter Conrad, *To Be Continued: Four Stories and Their Survival* (Oxford: Clarendon Press, 1995).

28 *The Annotated Frankenstein*.

29 Umberto Eco, *La Ricerca della lingua perfetta* (Rome and Bari: Editori Laterza, 1993).

30 G. K. Chesterton, *G. F. Watts* (London: Duckworth, 1914).

31 Death is the Monster's allotted place. Balderston's script carries a quotation from William Blake: 'So I turned to the Garden of Love/That so many sweet flowers bore;/And I saw it was filled with graves.'

32 Goethe, *Faust: Der Tragödie erster Teil*, line 334.

33 The painted limestone bust of Queen Nefertiti from the fourteenth century BC, now in the Egyptian Museum in Berlin, is one of the most famous icons of antiquity. The queen does not show a shock of hair like that of the Bride, but her headgear, rising high and slanted backwards, has the same general shape as that of her future sister. The strange beauty of these two famous women has often been compared.
34 Lanchester, *Elsa Lanchester Herself.*
35 Edward Field, 'The Bride of Frankenstein', in *Counting Myself Lucky: Selected Poems 1963–1992* (Santa Rosa, CA: Black Sparrow Press, 1992).
36 Forrest J. Ackerman, Foreword to *The Bride of Frankenstein: Original Shooting Script*, ed. Philip J. Riley (Abescon, NJ: MagicImage Filmbooks, 1989).
37 *Variety*, 15 May 1935.
38 Frank S. Nugent, 'Bride of Frankenstein', *New York Times*, 11 May 1935.
39 *Kinematograph Weekly*, 6 June 1935.
40 Aldous Huxley in his 1932 novel *Brave New World* imagines a future in which films will be grasped not only with eyes and ears but also with the senses of touch and smell.
41 The reference is to 'The Little Salamander' by Walter de la Mare, a short poem that ends: 'To see me in my bush of hair/Dance burning through the night.' In Walter de la Mare, *Collected Poems* (London: Faber, 1942).
42 Graham Greene, *Spectator*, 5 July 1935; reprinted in *The Pleasure-Dome: Graham Greene, The Collected Film Criticism 1935–1940* (London: Secker & Warburg, 1972).
43 Gershom Scholem, *Kabbalah* (New York: Dorset Press, 1974).

44 Quoted in Marc-Alain Ouaknin, *Le Livre brûlé: Philosophie du Talmud* (Paris: Editions du Seuil, 1986).
45 Mary Shelley, Introduction to *Frankenstein, or the Modern Prometheus* (London: 1931). (Not in the 1818 edition.)
46 Quoted in George Steiner, *The Death of Tragedy* (London: Faber, 1961).
47 Jorge Luis Borges, 'Los Precursuros de Kafka', in *Otras Inquisiciones* (Buenos Aires: Emecé, 1952).
48 Now in the Peggy Guggenheim Collection, Venice.
49 Though hair can also cover female nudity as to protect a woman from lascivious looks, as in the case of the repentant Mary Magdalen. 'Hair constantly reminds us of the closeness of the dumb animal in us, and we reveal our changing sympathies and values in the way we treat the relation, now relishing the animal in the human, now sternly denying it.' Marina Warner, 'The Language of Hair', in *From the Beast to the Blonde: On Fairytales and their Tellers* (London: Chatto & Windus, 1994).
50 Tristan Tzara, quoted in Neil Baldwin, *Man Ray* (London: Hamish Hamilton, 1989).
51 Pierre Cabanne, *Entretiens avec Marcel Duchamp* (Paris: Editions Pierre Belfond, 1967).
52 Richard Hamilton, *The Bride Stripped Bare By Her Bachelors, Even: A Typographic Version* (Stuttgart, London and Reykjavik: Editions Hansjörg Mayer, 1960).
53 Octavio Paz, 'La novia y sus solteros', in *Los Signos en rotación y otros ensayos* (Madrid: Alianza Editorial, 1971).

CREDITS

. . . .

Bride of Frankenstein

USA
1935
Production company
Universal Pictures
Corporation
Carl Laemmle, President
A James Whale Production
A Carl Laemmle
Production
US copyright
26 April 1935
US release
22 April 1935
US distributor
Universal Pictures
Corporation
UK tradeshow
28 May 1935
UK release
30 September 1935
UK distributor
Universal Pictures
Producer
Carl Laemmle Jr.
Director
James Whale
Assistant directors
Henry Mancke, Fred Frank,
Joseph McDonough
Screenplay
William Hurlbut.
Suggested by the novel
*Frankenstein, or, the Modern
Prometheus* by Mary
Wollstonecraft Shelley
Adaptation
William Hurlbut,
John Balderston
Script contribution
Tom Reed

Photography
John J. Mescall
2nd camera
Alan Jones
Assistant camera
William Dodds
Music
Franz Waxman
Orchestra conductor
Bakaleinikoff
Editor
Ted Kent
Supervising editor
Maurice J. Pivar
Art director
Charles D. Hall
Photography effects
John P. Fulton
Make-up
Jack Pierce, Otto Lederer
Sound supervisor
Gilbert Kurland
Doubles for
Ernest Thesiger
Peter Shaw, Monte
Montague
Double for
Reginald Barlow
George DeNormand
80 minutes
6,749 feet

[Boris] Karloff
The Monster
Colin Clive
Baron Henry Frankenstein
Valerie Hobson
Elizabeth
Ernest Thesiger
Doctor Pretorius
Elsa Lanchester
Mary Wollstonecraft
Shelley
Gavin Gordon
Lord Byron
Douglas Walton
Percy Bysshe Shelley
Una O'Connor
Minnie
E. E. Clive
Burgomaster
Lucien Prival
Albert, the butler
O. P. Heggie
Hermit
Dwight Frye
Karl, the hunchback
Reginald Barlow
Hans
Mary Gordon
Hans' wife
Ann Darling
Shepherdess
Ted Billings
Ludwig
?[Elsa Lanchester]
The Monster's mate
Joan Woodbury
Miniature Queen
Arthur S. Byron
Miniature King
Norman Ainsley
Miniature Archbishop
Peter Shaw
Miniature Devil
Kansas DeForrest
Miniature ballerina
Josephine McKim
Miniature mermaid

Robert A'Dair
Frank Terry
Hunters
Brenda Fowler
Mother
Helen Parrish
Communion girl
Walter Brennan
Rollo Lloyd
Mary Stewart
Neighbours
Gunnis Davis
Uncle Glutz

Tempe Pigott
Aunt Glutz
John Carradine
Jack Curtis
Hunters at hermit's hut
Neil Fitzgerald
Rudy, second graverobber
Sarah Schwartz
Marta
Edward Peil Sr.
Frank Benson
Anders Van Haden
John George
Villagers

Credits checked by Markku
Salmi. The print of *Bride
of Frankenstein* was
acquired specially for the
Treasures project from
Universal Pictures in Los
Angeles.

BIBLIOGRAPHY

Ackerman, Forrest J. (ed.). *Boris Karloff: The Frankenscience Monster* (New York: Ace, 1969).

Brunas, Michael, John Brunas and Tom Weaver. *Universal Horrors: The Studio's Classic Films 1931–46* (Jefferson, NC: McFarland & Co., 1990).

Conrad, Peter. *To Be Continued: Four Stories and Their Survival* (Oxford: Clarendon Press, 1995).

Curtis, James. *James Whale* (Metuchen, NJ and London: Scarecrow Press, 1982).

Fiedler, Leslie. *Freaks: Myths and Images of the Secret Self* (New York: Simon & Schuster, 1978).

Gardner, Gerald. *The Censorship Papers: Movie Censorship: Letters from the Hays Office 1934 to 1968* (New York: Dodd, Mead & Co., 1987).

Grylls, R. Glynn. *Mary Shelley: A Biography* (London, New York and Toronto: Oxford University Press, 1938).

Haining, Peter (ed.). *The Frankenstein Omnibus* (London: Orion Books, 1994).

Helman, Cecil. 'The Body of Frankenstein's Monster', in *Essays in Myth and Medicine* (New York and London: W. W. Norton & Co., 1991).

Hogan, David J. *Dark Romance: Sexuality in the Horror Film* (Jefferson, NC: McFarland & Co., 1986).

Lanchester, Elsa. *Elsa Lanchester Herself* (London: Michael Joseph, 1983).

Mank, Gregory William. *It's Alive! The Classic Cinema Saga of Frankenstein* (San Diego and New York: A. S. Barnes & Co., 1981).

Nollen, Scott Allen. *Boris Karloff: A Critical Account of His Screen, Stage, Radio, Television, and Recording Work* (Jefferson, NC and London: McFarland & Co., 1991).

Riley, Philip J. (ed.). *The Bride of Frankenstein: Original Shooting Script* (Abescon, NJ: MagicImage Filmbooks, 1989).

Shelley, Mary. *Frankenstein* (1818 edition), in *The Annotated Frankenstein*, with introduction and notes by Leonard Wolf (New York: 1977).

Shelley, Mary. *The Letters of Mary Shelley* (2 vols.), ed. Frederick L. Jones (University of Oklahoma Press, 1944).

Shelley, Mary. *Mary Shelley's Journal*, ed. Frederick L. Jones (University of Oklahoma Press, 1947).

Skal, David J. *The Monster Show: A Cultural History of Horror* (London: Plexus, 1993).

Sunstein, Emily W. *Mary Shelley: Romance and Reality* (Boston, Toronto and London: Little, Brown, 1989).

Tropp, Martin. *Mary Shelley's Monsters: The Story of Frankenstein* (Boston: Houghton Mifflin, 1976).

Underwood, Peter. *Karloff* (New York: Drake, 1972).

Wolf, Leonard. *Horror: A Connoisseur's Guide to Literature and Film* (New York and Oxford: Facts on File, 1989).

ALSO PUBLISHED

· ·

If you would like further information about future BFI Film Classics or about other books on film, media and popular culture from BFI Publishing, please write to:

BFI Film Classics
British Film Institute
21 Stephen Street
London
W1P 2LN

BFI FILM CLASSICS

THE BIG SLEEP

David Thomson

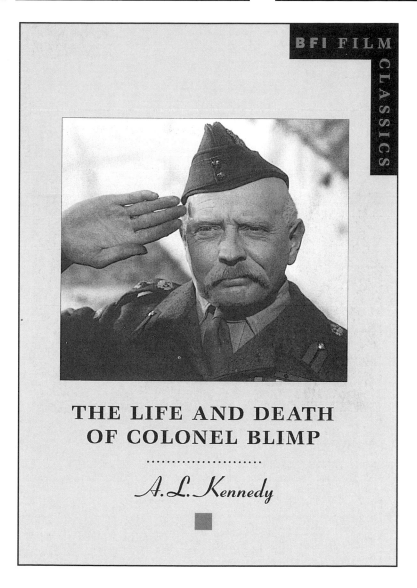

THE LIFE AND DEATH
OF COLONEL BLIMP

. . . .

A. L. Kennedy

"Film Classics - *one of the best ideas BFI Publishing has had*"
SUNDAY TIMES

BFI FILM CLASSICS

LES ENFANTS DU PARADIS

. . . .

Jill Forbes

"BFI Film Classics ... *could scarcely be improved upon ...*
informative , intelligent, jargon-free companions"
THE OBSERVER

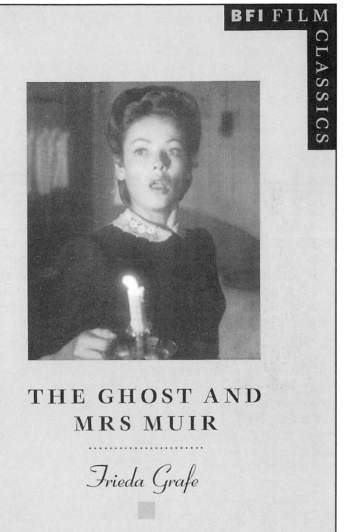

BFI FILM
CLASSICS

THE GHOST AND
MRS MUIR

. . . .

Frieda Grafe

"elegant and intriguing"
SIGHT AND SOUND

BFI FILM CLASSICS

BFI FILM CLASSICS

THE WIZARD OF OZ

. . . .

Salman Rushdie

"Witty and vivacious ... shrewd and joyous ...
it adds to the movie's wonder, which is saying a lot"
NEW STATESMAN

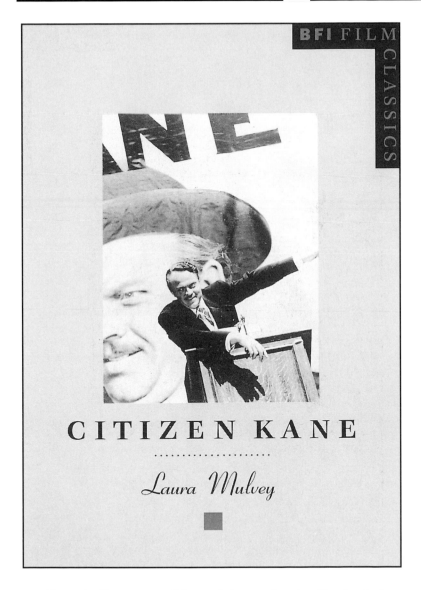

BFI FILM
CLASSICS

CITIZEN KANE

Laura Mulvey

"An enthralling account of the movie by one of our best film theorists"
THE GUARDIAN

Each book in the BFI Film Classics series honours a great film from the history of world cinema. With four new titles published each spring and autumn, the series will rapidly build into a collection representing some of the best writing on film. Forthcoming titles include *Citizen Kane* by Laura Mulvey, *The Big Heat* by Colin McArthur, *Brief Encounter* by Richard Dyer and *L'Atalante* by Marina Warner.

If you would like to receive further information about future BFI Film Classics or about other books on film, media and popular culture from BFI Publishing, please fill in your name and address below and return the card to the BFI.

No stamp is needed if posted in the United Kingdom, Channel Islands, or Isle of Man.

NAME

ADDRESS

POSTCODE

**BFI Publishing
21 Stephen Street
FREEPOST 7
LONDON
W1E 4AN**